To Dr. Gearhart,

In appreciation for all you
do to make a difference.

Gratefully,
Susan L. Garbett

CONFRONTING CHORDOMA CANCER

An Uncommon Journey

Susan L. Garbett

Published in the United States by:

Parquetry Press
P.O. Box 1694
Tallevast, FL 34270

This is a true story. Some names have been changed to respect individual privacy.

The views in this book are solely those of the author and were not intended to present medical, legal or financial advice. If such assistance or advice is required, a competent professional should be consulted.

Every effort has been made to provide accurate resources; however, because of the nature of the Internet, the web addresses and links cited in this book may have changed since publication and may no longer be valid. Neither the publisher nor the author assumes any responsibility for errors or changes that occur after publication. In addition, the publisher does not have any control over, and does not assume any responsibility for author or third party websites or their content.

Cover art by Janet B. Mishner

Printed in the United States of America

ISBN 978-0-9836171-9-8

Published in partnership with Suncoast Digital Press, Inc.
Sarasota, Florida

This book is gratefully dedicated to
Jean-Paul Wolinsky, M.D.
Norbert J. Liebsch, M. D.
whose devotion to helping their patients
and furthering medical advancement is extraordinary.

The Chordoma Foundation
for their continued commitment to research and education.

The American Cancer Society
The AstraZeneca Hope Lodge Center in Boston
for their dedication in helping people with cancer
through education, treatment, and patient services.

ACKNOWLEDGMENTS

I could not have made it through the journey or written this book alone. There are many people to *THANK*:

- The many talented and skilled physicians, nurses, and medical personnel I had the pleasure to meet over the years. I am indebted to all of you for your help and your commitment to your patients.

- All those people I know, and all those I never met, for their outpouring of love and for their prayers that were said on my behalf.

- Everyone who reviewed sections of this book for accuracy and clarity. I appreciate your time and effort.

- Dr. Jean-Paul Wolinsky for writing the foreword for this book.

- The Hackerman-Patz Pavilion at Johns Hopkins, and the AstraZeneca Hope Lodge Center in Boston, which provided a "home away from home" that helped ease the financial burden throughout this long journey.

- The friends I met at the Hope Lodge, who will stay in my heart forever.

- Adeline Silverman, my initial editor, for her insight and believing I had a story to tell.

- Janet Mishner, an incredible artist and dear friend, who designed the book cover.

- Barbara Dee, at Suncoast Digital Press, for her editing, guidance and vision with publishing this book.

- My husband, Chuck, for loving me, believing in me, supporting me, and being my cheerleader in all that I do.

Contents

Foreword ix

Preface xi

Part One: Accepting the New Reality

1. This is a Big Deal 3
2. Decisions...Decisions...Decisions 15
3. Baltimore 23
4. The Focus 33
5. No Turning Back .43
6. Can Anybody Hear Me? 47
7. This Is Not Working! 51
8. I'm Not Oriental .57
9. On to Rehab 63
10. Push the Easy Button 69
11. Breakfast Club 77
12. Finally! 85
13. More Historic News 89
14. "Meanwhile, I Keep Dancing" 95
15. Something's Not Right 103
16. No More Food Commercials 113
17. Music to My Ears 119
18. Last Week in Baltimore 123
19. It's the Little Things 133
20. Remembrance 137
21. Tuesdays with Janet 141
22. A Sigh of Relief 149
23. Get Several Sheets of Paper 157
24. Where to stay? 163

Part Two: Unexpected Warmth in Boston's Chill

25. "No worry lines and no wrinkles!" 169
26. A Home Away From Home 175
27. A Powerful Gift 183
28. Generosity Abounds 189
29. Bonding at Hope Lodge 195
30. Amazing Technology 203
31. That Look 213
32. A Delightful Surprise 217
33. The Dream 225
34. Patience! 231
35. A Bell-Ringing Triumph 235

Epilogue 241

Resources 245

About the Author 247

Foreword

Susan Garbett is neither unfamiliar with the medical system nor a newcomer to being diagnosed with various ailments. Still, this did not prepare her for being diagnosed with a rare tumor—a tumor she had never heard of, a tumor some of her doctors were unfamiliar with, a tumor few had experience treating.

She takes us through this frightening and confusing journey from the perspective of a patient. Her journey highlights her perseverance and demonstrates the wonderful support she receives from her family, friends, other patients and, most of all, her loving husband. Although her story is about her experience with a chordoma, this is not a story about a specific, rare tumor. It is the story of courage and grit in the face of an unknown challenger. This is a story of empowerment through self-reliance and knowledge.

Jean-Paul Wolinsky, M.D.
Associate Professor of Neurosurgery and Oncology
Clinical Director of the Neurosurgery Spine Program
Johns Hopkins University/Hospital

Preface

As I considered writing this book, I found that two questions dominated my decision process: *Does anyone want to read another book about cancer? Am I willing to expose myself publicly, opening up this private part of me and sharing my personal journey?* As words became paragraphs and the paragraphs became pages, I realized I had a story that needed to be told, especially since very little has been written about chordomas, particularly from the patient's perspective.

My goal in writing *Confronting Chordoma Cancer; An Uncommon Journey* is not only to bring awareness to this little known and very rare form of cancer, but also to help empower people struggling with the uncomfortable realities and consequences of chordomas and other types of cancer, by providing stress management techniques and strategies that worked well for me. This book is not intended to be a medical document, although all the physicians named in this book have approved their sections for accuracy and clarity. It is meant to be a candid, self-reflective account that presents the paradox between sadness and joy, pain and contentment, heartbreak and elation, despair and hope for those with serious illness, but also for anyone facing a huge challenge and those close to them.

—Susan L. Garbett

You may encounter many defeats,
But you must not be defeated.
In fact, it might be necessary
to encounter defeats,
so you can know who you are,
what you can rise from,
how you can still come out of it.

—Maya Angelou

PART ONE

Accepting the
New Reality

1

This is a Big Deal

S CANNING THE NEATLY ARRANGED ROWS of multi-patterned chairs in this massive waiting room, I spotted my husband, Chuck, walking towards me.

"How was it?" he asked.

"An EMG [electromyography] has never been my favorite test. The electrode part isn't bad, but when they insert those small needles into your muscles, it's really hard to relax. They have a different concept of what *small* is. It's painful and I'm just glad it's over."

"Dr. Calamia's secretary just called me and asked us to come to his office as soon as you were finished," Chuck said.

"He must want to get out of Dodge early and get a head start on the Fourth of July holiday weekend," I replied.

We were kept waiting for only a few minutes before Dr. Calamia, wearing a pin-striped shirt and sporting a bright royal-blue patterned bow tie, entered the room. He greeted us with a friendly smile and handshake, and promptly proceeded to scan his computer, apparently searching for my test and lab results. I was so impressed with the efficiency of the Mayo Clinic here in Jacksonville, Florida. We had always heard great things about Mayo, but it was only after experiencing its way of doing things for a few days that we realized their competency went way beyond our expectations.

"Your blood work and bone scan both look fine," he said. "Radiology found something on your MRI [magnetic resonance imaging] that we need to address." Without any hesitation and looking directly at us, he said, "Our radiology team discovered a sacral chordoma rising from the sacrum about the size of a baseball."

"A what?" I said. "Never heard of it. How do you spell it?" My mind was spinning, but I knew Chuck was taking notes. We serve as each other's recording secretary at most medical appointments. Using a calm and reassuring tone, Dr. Calamia explained that a sacral chordoma is a rare, malignant boney tumor in the sacral area of the spine.

Stunned, it took a minute or so before I could get a word out. "I heard *malignant* and *rare*. I understand malignant, but what are you talking about when you say rare?"

"One in a million," Dr. Calamia responded.

I didn't speak. His words sucked the air out of my lungs. I felt tightness in my throat. As I tried to digest Dr. Calamia's words, I felt Chuck's hand close over mine. Silence filled the room. As my heart sank in this small office, I had a sense Chuck's heart was sinking in unison with mine. My mind began to race. *How can this be happening? This is unbelievable. I came to the Mayo Clinic for a routine rheumatology evaluation for lupus and a few other autoimmune conditions, and now this doctor is telling me I have a rare cancer. And here I thought he wanted to see us early so he could get a head start on his holiday vacation.*

I took a deep breath and finally had the courage to turn and face Chuck. As I leaned my head on his shoulder, I heard him whisper in my ear, "We'll get through this." Dr. Calamia didn't rush us. His patient understanding gave us time to absorb what he had just told us. This merciful pause was exactly what we needed.

"Of course, we can't be absolutely sure until we have a biopsy confirming our diagnosis," he said, "but your scan was thoroughly analyzed by some of the top radiologists in the country. I have already made an appointment for you to see Dr. Mary O'Connor, an orthopedic oncologist familiar with chordomas tomorrow at five o'clock. Your test results and my notes are already in the Mayo computer system, so she will be able to review your file before you arrive. Do you have any questions?" *What? I wanted to scream. Of course I have questions. Lots of them, but having never heard of this type of tumor, I didn't even know what to ask. I felt a bit stupid and at a loss for words, which, as Chuck will attest to, is a rare occurrence.*

After a long spell, I began to speak. "Would this explain the coccyx pain that I've suffered with for several years? Could this have been caused from having fractured my tailbone while riding the log flume at Hershey Amusement Park five consecutive times with our grandson?"

"It didn't help the situation any, but it certainly didn't cause it," Dr. Calamia replied. A chordoma is a cancer that develops from remnants of embryonic notochord in the skull-base or spine."

"Are you saying that I was born with this?" I asked.

"Yes," he replied.

My thoughts became mush. *This is mind-boggling! I knew I didn't fully comprehend all that was being said. The only thing I could think of was that I'm glad my father isn't alive, because he would be beside himself if he thought for a moment I could have possibly inherited this condition from him.*

"Dr. O'Connor will be able to address your questions more adequately when you see her tomorrow," Dr. Calamia said.

Chuck and I stood, exchanged pleasantries and thanked Dr. Calamia. He told us we could stay in this room as we try to regain our composure if we wanted to, since no other patients were scheduled today. As the door closed behind him, Chuck took me in his arms. Feeling his strength supporting me gave me the courage to pull away slightly and to look him in the eye. His vivid baby blues were teary-eyed, and I began to feel wet streaks running down my cheeks. Chuck gently brushed and kissed them away.

"Let's get out of here," I said.

Returning to the Wingate Hotel after a delicious dinner at a quaint restaurant on the north side of Jacksonville, I found a computer located off to the side of the hotel lobby. Googling *chordoma,* I quickly scanned the links that appeared. I had mentally debated whether or not to delve into this unfamiliar world of chordomas, knowing too much information could be overwhelming and upsetting. But how else was I going to ask intelligent questions at tomorrow's appointment? I began reading the overview I found on the Chordoma Foundation website: http://www.chordomafoundation.org

There was a wealth of information, including descriptions, sub-types, statistics, percentages, etc. One section talked about how chordomas can often be misdiagnosed because of being confused with other types of tumors.

I stopped reading at *Prognosis and Survival.* I had a general idea what this new term meant, but did not want to drive myself crazy with a bunch of details and worst-case scenarios that might not pertain to me. I took notes as I read and re-read the information for better understanding to hopefully help my brain summarize and focus only on the material unique to my type of chordoma.

I learned that chordomas are a rare malignant cancer that occurs in the bones of the skull and spine. In the United States, there are around 300 new cases of chordoma diagnosed each year, which is approximately one new case per million people. Chordomas can appear anywhere along the spine, from the head to the tailbone. They are generally slow growing, but are relentless and tend to recur after treatment. This type of tumor can occur in people of all ages, from infants to the elderly. The median age of diagnosis is forty-nine for skull-based chordomas and sixty-nine for sacral chordomas. *Well, at sixty-one, I guess I'm not too far off the mark.*

I continued to study the Chordoma Foundation web site, relieved that at least I had this valuable source of information. I learned that chordomas are thought to arise from remnants of the embryonic notochord, a rod-shaped, cartilage-like structure that serves as a scaffold for the formation of the spinal column. Notochord cells normally persist after birth, lodged inside the spine and skull. In very rare cases, these cells undergo a malignant transformation which leads to the formation of a chordoma.

My brain was on overload, saturated with almost too much information, some easily understandable, other details unfamiliar medical jargon. Dr. Calamia had sincerely tried to explain my condition, trying not to overwhelm or frighten me anymore than necessary. He was not entirely successful since this was the most terrifying thing I ever had to face in my life. The most significant thing I learned from the Chordoma Foundation website was how important it was to get multiple opinions from experienced pathologists who routinely see these types of tumors before proceeding with any treatment. Exhausted and drained, I printed out my notes and decided to wait to talk to Dr. O'Connor about the specifics of my case the following afternoon.

A small-framed, attractive blond woman, dressed in a white lab coat, was sitting at her computer desk as Chuck and I were escorted into her office. Dr. O'Connor immediately stood and welcomed us. Ushering us over to the upholstered sofa, she pulled her chair over to be closer to where we were seated.

"I've talked to Dr. Calamia and have reviewed the records and information you brought with you, as well as the tests and labs we did here at Mayo this week," she began. "I have also personally reviewed your CT [computerized tomography] of the pelvis and your MRI with Dr. Kransdorf, a radiologist on staff here. What have you been told about sacral chordomas?"

I gave Dr. O'Connor a brief synopsis of what I had read, and expressed my reluctance about going online to get more information I knew I probably wouldn't understand without consulting with her first. She elaborated a little more on what I had just told her, letting us know, in her opinion, surgery to remove the tumor was the best option in my case.

Then Dr. O'Connor said, "Assuming this is a sacral chordoma, you will require a surgical resection that will be a major operative undertaking. This is a complicated and extensive surgery, requiring a multi-disciplinary team, including an orthopedic surgeon, a neurosurgeon, a vascular surgeon, a plastic surgeon, and a colon-rectal surgeon. I believe this would best be served by a combined anterior and posterior approach, meaning going in from both the front and the back."

In my mind I imagined an operating room, jam-packed with doctors in scrubs. I could not fully process what she had said, confused as to whether I should picture myself face-up or face-down on the operating table in the midst of my "team."

"There are no guarantees and there are many complications that could arise. There is a strong possibility that you may have bowel and bladder functional loss, as I am not sure if the S2 and S3 nerve roots can be preserved if we're going to be successful in removing the entire tumor." She paused. "The good thing about a chordoma is you won't have to have chemo, because this type of tumor doesn't respond to chemotherapy." *Is she for real? I thought most cancers were treated with a combination of chemo and radiation.*

Dr. O'Connor continued, "Another big plus that we learned from today's PET [positron emission tomography] and CT scans is that there is no evidence of hypermetabolic activity anywhere in your body, meaning the cancer is localized to that one area. Of course, we will need to do a biopsy to confirm our diagnosis.

Unfortunately, we are closed tomorrow and the weekend, so it can't be scheduled until next week."

This was too much to take in. As I watched Chuck writing feverishly in his notebook, all I could think of was how much all of this was going to cost. *That's ridiculous, Susan; this is your life she's talking about. Get a grip.* I didn't want to get a grip. I just wanted to go back to Sarasota and go back to the life Chuck and I had before we came to Mayo. I closed my eyes, took a deep breath, trying to make sense of it all and hoping this would jar me back to reality.

Dr. O'Connor sensed that I wasn't getting it. "Susan, this is a big deal!" Her words were like the proverbial velvet hammer. She was making a strong point, yet it was underlined with compassion. She did not rush me, and allowed me time to absorb the shock of what she was saying. I glanced at Chuck, who looked as dumbstruck as I felt.

"The word **cancer** is just so foreign," I said. "It's hard for me to wrap my brain around the word, much less one that is so rare. I don't think anyone on either side of my family has had any type of cancer." I guess just saying the word *cancer* freed me, and the questions began to flow.

"So if you have to cut the nerves that control the bowel and bladder, what does that mean?" I asked.

"You will have to catheterize yourself to urinate, and will have to stick your finger up your butt to evacuate." My mind screamed. *This is getting more frightening by the minute!*

"What's the usual recovery time for chordoma surgery?" I asked.

"It's different with every patient, depending on the outcome and if there are no complications, but you can figure on six months to a year before you are feeling like yourself again," Dr. O'Connor said. "Don't get too far ahead of yourself too soon."

After answering all the questions I was firing at her and also the ones Chuck had, she again reminded us of the enormity of the situation. "Like I said, Susan, this is a big deal!"

I liked her. She was professional, knowledgeable, and compassionate, exuding confidence and making us feel she had all the time in the world to address our concerns. She was a straight-shooter, yet her warmth and sincerity made you feel like you were talking to your neighbor. I was grateful that she was spending so much time with us.

Suddenly, a disturbing thought crossed my mind. "Dr. O'Connor, do you think this sacral chordoma could be the perineural cyst the orthopedist and radiologist found on the MRI done in Sarasota over a year and a half ago? I was also evaluated by a neurosurgeon who agreed my MRI showed a perineural cyst. His recommendation was to 'leave it alone' because removing it might cause infection and more problems, and there could still be a chance that the cyst would grow back."

Dr. O'Connor replied, "I definitely do, since our radiology team and I have reviewed both MRIs and compared the two. What they were calling a large perineural cyst was actually a sacral chordoma arising from the S4-S5 region. The tumor has almost doubled in size since then. You have to remember this is a very rare tumor and many doctors are not familiar with them."

I heard what Dr. O'Connor was tactfully trying to say; *I was misdiagnosed in Sarasota.* I was trying to think rationally. Most physicians may have learned about sacral chordomas in medical school, but years later, because of their rarity, there is a real probability they wouldn't be recognized as the life changer they are, or the potential killer they could be. There was a limit to my understanding, but knowing my tumor had almost doubled in size due to their error, making it a lot more difficult to remove without severing those nerves, caused incredible anger and fear to well up in me. *Susan, you can't go backwards. Try to put the word "incontinence" out of your mind. You really have to concentrate on the present and move forward.*

I told Dr. O'Connor the most important thing I learned from the Chordoma Foundation website was to at least get a second opinion.

"That's absolutely right," she said. "And I will be glad to forward your records to any physician of your choosing."

"How many chordoma surgeries have you done?" I asked.

She answered, "Six to eight."

What? You can't remember if it was six, seven, or eight? No matter what she remembers, that certainly didn't seem like enough experience to me, even though I really liked her.

"Where would you suggest I go for a second opinion?" I asked.

"If it were me, I would recommend going to the Mayo Clinic in Rochester, Minnesota. Their team has done many more chordoma surgeries than I have, and I think you will be very pleased with the docs up there. I'll give you two names and phone numbers of physicians in Rochester. My secretary will call you when the biopsy is scheduled, which I will try to expedite. I'll call you as soon as I get the results."

"What about Johns Hopkins?" I asked. "I lived in Baltimore for almost sixty years before moving to Sarasota two years ago. I have a long medical history with Hopkins and my family and friends live there."

"Johns Hopkins is excellent," she said. "I can give you the name of an orthopedic surgeon there if you would like."

I glanced at my watch. It was seven o'clock. Dr. O'Connor had been with us for almost two hours. I was so impressed with her compassion and professionalism. She is truly a class act!

"Enjoy the holiday," Dr. O'Connor said before we left her office. "I'll be in touch."

Walking towards the elevator, I turned to Chuck and said, "I guess my book isn't going to get published this summer."

Seeing the disappointment on my face, he replied, "Probably not, but knowing you, I'm confident as soon as you feel up to it, you'll set the wheels in motion again."

I knew he was right, but so much of my time and energy had been focused on writing *Susie and Me: Joy in the Shadow of Dementia*, it was frustrating and depressing to realize I now had a new and unwelcome set of priorities and steps which would consume my attention for who knew how long.

Exiting the elevator on the ground level, we noticed the halls were empty. It was very eerie, so unlike the hubbub and babbling of languages heard earlier in the day. We did see two people as we walked from the clinic to what now was an almost empty parking lot. Before opening my car door, Chuck embraced me with an intensity that was overpowering, and yet comforting. *I am so blessed to have him in my life. I can't imagine facing this alone.*

I called my cousin, Michael, as Chuck was pulling out of the parking lot. He is an internist and cardiologist at New York Presbyterian Hospital, Columbia University Medical Center. He is also our family's "go to" person for clarification on all medical issues and terms we don't understand. He's a gem and a fabulous physician, and I was thrilled when Arleen, his wife, answered the phone.

"Hi Ar," I said, "I'm so glad you're home."

"Susie, it's nice to hear your voice. How is everything?" she asked.

"Okay," I replied, knowing that wasn't really true. "Chuck and I are just leaving the Mayo Clinic in Jacksonville and I have some important questions to ask Michael. If he is there and can pick up on another phone, I'll fill you both in at the same time."

Taking a deep breath and trying not to sound too upset, I began to give my cousins a thumb-nail sketch of what had just transpired at the Mayo Clinic.

"Oh my goodness, Susie," they both said almost simultaneously.

"All of this hasn't really sunk in for either of us yet," I said, "but we both know we want to get at least one other opinion. I'm trying to decide where to have this surgery done and which doctor to do it. Chuck and I both really liked the orthopedic oncologist at Mayo, but she told us she had only performed six to eight of these type surgeries. That didn't seem like very many, and we really want to find the best surgeon out there who has the most experience with sacral chordomas. We don't know exactly where to start, but the Chordoma Foundation website listed several neurosurgeons who specialize in this area."

I relayed what Dr. O'Connor had told us about going to the Mayo Clinic in Rochester.

Michael spoke up and said, "Susie, you're not going to find a surgeon that has done a thousand of these, since they are so rare. I will make some inquires up here at Columbia after the holiday weekend, and I will definitely get back to you as soon as I have more information."

"Thanks Michael, I really appreciate it. All the other medical issues I've called you about over the years seem so trite compared to this one. Please do me a big favor and don't say anything to anyone yet, not until I have a chance to talk to Craig and Scott (my children). I have to have time to digest this some more and find the right words, so I can calmly tell them that their mother has a very rare cancer."

"Of course we will respect your wishes," Ar said. "Just let us know if we can help in any way. We're here for you and Chuck."

Michael said, "I'll try to call you Monday or Tuesday of next week. Don't hesitate to call me if you have any other questions or concerns. Have a safe trip home and I'll be in touch."

13

Closing my cell phone, I looked over at Chuck who was focused on driving through the maze of heavy holiday traffic. Since I had my phone on speaker, I knew he had heard everything Michael had said.

"Sugah, we'll talk when we get back to the motel."

I agreed it was probably better that we didn't discuss this while Chuck was driving. As I gazed absently out the car window, a myriad of thoughts ran through my mind. I felt tears pooling in my eyes. The drama that had unfolded during the past two days felt surreal. My stomach was tied in knots.

Initially I was surprised that I was even able to get an appointment at Mayo on my own, much less getting one within three weeks after contacting their Rheumatology Department. I had always had the impression that to get an appointment at the prestigious Mayo Clinic you had to have a referral from a specialist or have a condition so rare that most people have never heard of it, and probably couldn't pronounce or spell it. I realized now with my diagnosis of a sacral chordoma, I truly fit my own criterion.

2

Decisions...Decisions...Decisions

THE FOURTH OF JULY WEEKEND crept by ever so slowly. The reality of my latest medical news, along with the anxiety of the upcoming biopsy, forced us to cancel plans with friends. Going would mean wearing a false smile and listening to everyone's gay chatter. We both knew we would have a hard time keeping up a pretense that it was "business as usual." For us, nothing could be further from the truth. We chose instead to spend a quiet weekend together without all the hoopla and expectations that Independence Day usually brings.

Chuck and I were each trying to be strong for one another, carefully choosing our words, not wanting to cause any further upset or distress. At times I found the silence between us comforting, the unspoken word calming, as we sat together listening to Andrea Bocelli fill our home with light operatic beauty.

This serenity was certainly needed but was short-lived. It wasn't enough to overcome the turmoil and uncertainty within. After the initial shock, the enormity of this complicated surgery and the possible outcomes were beginning to sink in. I realized that, even if the surgical team was able to remove the tumor, there was a good possibility I would be left without normal bowel and/ or bladder function.

Solace and a sense of inner peace came when I started saying the *Modeh Ani*, a Hebrew prayer that is said upon arising each

15

morning. Over the years I had gotten away from reciting it, too eager to start my day, too busy to focus on its meaning.

I offer thanks to You, living and eternal King, for You have restored my soul within me: Your faithfulness is great.

Now, faced with such uncertainty and so many unanswered questions, this simple prayer spoke to me, and every morning it became my first conscious act, thanking God for the gift of life.

I knew the phone calls to our children would be difficult. I took time to gather my thoughts, trying to find the right words to ease the shock of what I was about to tell them. I wrote a brief crib sheet with a few key points that I wanted to get across. It was a good exercise for me, although I knew prolonging the inevitable was making it harder. Even though my two sons and Chuck's daughter and son were all adults, my maternal instincts made me want to protect them. I thought about contacting them through Skype, but decided against the idea because I wasn't sure if I could keep my emotions under control. I wished I could make a conference call so I would only have to say this once.

Their loving support was overwhelming, at times making it harder for me to hold it together. They listened intently and said all the right things. "We're here for you, Mom. You'll get through this," Scott said in an unusually subdued tone. Craig kept emphasizing, "I'll be there no matter where you have the surgery, Mom. Try not to worry."

Chuck called his children to ease the burden on me. I watched him as he sat on a chair on our lanai with his back toward me. Later, he told me Chris and Buddy expressed similar sentiments. Buddy, who sells orthopedic appliances and goes into the operating room with the orthopedists in Virginia, said he would ask the "docs" he knew and do some research on his own to find surgeons most familiar with chordomas.

I had a gut feeling that after each conversation, all of them would be on their laptop, Blackberry, or iPhone googling *chordoma* to find out more information. We asked everyone to keep this information confidential until after the biopsy actually confirmed the diagnosis. No sense getting everyone upset until the diagnosis was definitely confirmed. In my heart of hearts I knew the diagnosis was correct. I remembered Mayor Rudy Giuliani's accusatory words after the 1993 World Trade Center bombing when he said, "If it looks like a bomb, smells like a bomb, it must be a bomb!" *What made me think of that?*

Over the weekend we diligently continued to research the Doctor's Database on The Chordoma Foundation website. We developed a list of medical specialists, sorted by location and fields of expertise, including skull base and spine neurosurgeons, otolaryngologist/ENT surgeons, orthopedic surgeons, and medical and radiation oncologists. This list provided the most valuable information for us to review. Although our focus was on practicing physicians at the Mayo Clinic in Rochester and at Johns Hopkins Hospital in Baltimore, we didn't limit our search to just those two hospitals. We were willing to travel anywhere in the United States to consult with the best specialist. After we compiled the initial list, we researched each doctor's credentials on their particular hospital's website to obtain more information. Our search was time-consuming, but worth the effort.

Having lived in Baltimore most of my life, it was only natural for us to think of Johns Hopkins first. It was where many of my current doctors practiced, and where I went for most of my tests, procedures, and hospital admissions. Although we were novices at this, we liked the description we found about the Johns Hopkins Spine Center:

> The Spine Center at Johns Hopkins has vast experience with sacral chordomas, which has allowed us to develop a comprehensive philosophy for their treatment. Because

these tumors metastasize, the first operative intervention provides the best chance for cure and control of the tumor. In addition, surgical en-bloc resection provides overall increased survival and tumor control. Because chordomas are fairly rare, success is achieved best through a team approach to treatment by a highly experienced group of physicians. Treatment involves preoperative planning, surgical resection, and postoperative therapy.

There were fourteen neurosurgeons on our list of specialists in chordoma surgery. We meticulously evaluated each one comparing education, certifications, and fields of interest. We narrowed our choices to five and decided to wait to hear from Michael and Buddy to see if the names of any of these doctors matched the ones recommended from responses to their inquiries.

My cousin Arleen sent me an email gently reminding me my support team of family and friends was in Baltimore, pointing out the long and possibly tough recovery period after the surgery. She wrote, "How many people do you know in Rochester, Minnesota?"

On Monday, Arleen called to tell me Michael had just returned to the office and had made some inquires and had spoken to the Chief of Neurosurgery at the New York Presbyterian Hospital, Columbia University Medical Center. She gave me the name of Dr. Ziya Gokaslan and then told me how to spell it. "Thanks Ar, and please thank Michael for us." Later that evening, Buddy called with the same neurosurgeon, which coincidently was on the top-five list Chuck and I had developed. Dr. Gokaslan practices at Johns Hopkins. *Fantastic!*

First thing the next morning, I called Johns Hopkins to schedule an appointment even before the biopsy was performed. We were eager to get started and just figured it would take some time to get an appointment. To my surprise, the secretary told me my records had to be reviewed and I had to be accepted before making an appointment. *Wow, I certainly wasn't prepared for that response.* She was specific as to what information should be faxed to them. I told her I was sure I could have them faxed that day and to please call me on my cell when their evaluation was complete.

I was sure Dr. O'Connor's office could fax my records to Hopkins that day, but I was glad we took the time to pick up my daily reports and test results from Mayo's Release of Information Health Services office before we left for Sarasota. I feel it's so important to be your own strongest advocate when it comes to medical matters and to obtain and maintain copies of all your test results, doctor's reports, and health information. The more information you can put your fingers on, the better. This has proven invaluable to me time and time again.

Then came the real kicker. "Dr. Gokaslan has opted out of participating in any health insurance," the secretary told me. I was stunned! *What? Is this for real? I knew about "designer" doctors and I had heard that many doctors were not accepting any type of insurance, but this is Hopkins, one of the world's preeminent health care institutions, acclaimed around the world for setting the standard of excellence in patient care for everyone. What's happening here?*

I asked what his initial consultation fee would be and her candid answer concluded with "...you have to pay up front before you can be seen." Again, I was just floored. *What? I don't pay for most things before I receive the service, even my dry cleaning!*

I realized that now Chuck and I had some really tough decisions to make. This was going to be a game changer no matter the outcome. Things would never be the same again.

Chuck decided that Dr. Gokaslan was considered *the* premier expert when it came to the surgical removal of spinal tumors and complex spinal reconstructions in the U.S. We read that he had developed novel surgical methods to treat some of the most difficult types of spinal cancers. Chuck said, "Sugah, we want the best neurosurgeon we can find to perform this surgery. I think we should set up a consultation so he can evaluate you. That's what a second opinion is all about."

"But how are we going to afford this guy?" I asked him.

"We'll worry about that if and when we get to schedule an appointment with him."

"Look, I want the best, also," I said, "but not if it's going to ruin us financially."

Chuck replied, "Let's cross that bridge when we come to it."

Looking back, I see that there was still an element of denial about the seriousness of my situation. I was thinking in an old paradigm, a box where decisions are weighed with cost/benefit analysis. Without saying so directly, Chuck knew that when it comes to life or death — plans, practices and priorities change. We would proceed to find the best.

Any apprehension about having the biopsy melted away after the Mayo doctor in Jacksonville discussed the benefits and risks of the procedure, going over in great detail exactly what she was going to do. I would be placed in a prone position, and would be prepped with a local anesthetic to numb the area. Using CT imagery to target the mass in the midline sacrum, I would feel pressure from the biopsy needle and hear a "snap", indicating she had the samples she needed. Afterwards the specimen would be reviewed thoroughly by a pathologist, but in my case, because my chordoma was so rare, she felt sure that a team of pathologists would be examining my tissue.

The actual biopsy procedure turned out to be no big deal, and actually not much different from the numerous nerve blocks I've had over the years to treat chronic regional pain syndrome, a condition I have resulting from back surgery. Lying on your stomach is a real plus, since you never really see what the doctor is doing or the size of the needle. All those scary thoughts of this gigantic needle that kept surfacing were unfounded.

Leaving Mayo, I checked my phone for messages. There was a voice mail from the secretary at Johns Hopkins letting me know I had been accepted and that I had an appointment with Dr. Gokaslan in a week. That was unbelievably quick. I thought about what Buddy had told me, "Just remember these docs want you. They love a challenge. In fact, some of them thrive on it."

The phone call from Dr. O'Connor came three days later, on a Saturday. I was so impressed she didn't wait until Monday to give us the report. After Chuck picked up the phone in the den, Dr. O' Connor told us that the biopsy confirmed the diagnosis, "positive for malignancy consistent with chordoma." Dr. O'Connor patiently answered all our questions, again emphasizing the enormity of this type of surgery. She was already aware that my records had been faxed to Johns Hopkins for review by their neurosurgery team. I told her I already had made an appointment with a neurosurgeon at the Johns Hopkins Spine Center for next Thursday. Before she hung up, she wished us well and said not to hesitate to contact her if we needed anything else. We both thanked her for her expertise, understanding, candor and patience. She was just wonderful.

I realized how fortunate we were. Being retired enabled us to pick up and go wherever with only a few disruptions to our lives. I can't imagine how hard it must be for someone who works every day, has children at home, or doesn't have the financial assets to travel such long distances.

And now I had to let everyone know.

July 12

Dear Family and Friends,

Chuck and I went to the Mayo Clinic in Jacksonville at the end of June to confer with a rheumatologist, at the suggestion of my rheumatologist in Baltimore and my internist in Sarasota. It is an amazing place, extremely efficient, professional, with quality top-notch doctors. I was very pleased with the rheumatologist I saw. After three days of tests, their team concluded that I have a sacral chordoma, a very rare malignant tumor, rising from the sacrum which has increased in size from the MRI done last year.

This tumor will require a difficult surgery involving an orthopedic surgeon, neurosurgeon, vascular surgeon, and colon rectal surgeon. An orthopedic oncologist at Mayo said this is an all-day procedure, and they would be going in from both the front and back. There is a strong possibility of loss of bladder and bowel function as a result of the surgery.

A few days ago I went back to Mayo for a needle biopsy. My orthopedic oncologist called this morning and confirmed the diagnosis of sacral chordoma. She was wonderful, and spent a great deal of time answering my long list of questions.

So we're off to Baltimore Wednesday, and will get another opinion from Johns Hopkins on Thursday. Then we will have some huge decisions to make.

There are some things working in my favor:

- *I'm in relatively good health. (No heart disease, diabetes, etc.)*
- *The PET scan showed that the cancer hasn't spread.*
- *I will not need chemo!*

The enormity and challenge of this type of surgery is just beginning to sink in and is quite scary. Since there is no history of cancer on either side of my family, this came as quite a shock.

That's it for now. I'll keep you posted.

Hope everyone is having a nice summer.

Love to all,

Susan

3

Baltimore

S ITTING QUIETLY IN THE WAITING area at the Southwest terminal in Tampa was a welcome change from the crazy pace both of us had been keeping while trying to get ready to leave for Baltimore. With just a week's notice, we had quite an extensive to-do list of personal, medical, financial, and home-related items to take care of. As each day passed, it was gratifying to scratch items off one at a time and see the list shrink. In some ways it was a blessing to be so busy, our focus being on what needed to be taken care of, not on what lay ahead. Our wonderful neighbor, Cay, offered to watch our house, water the plants, and forward any mail that looked important. Thank goodness for online bill pay. This made everything so much faster and easier. Chuck carefully closed all the hurricane shutters before our friends, Jeanne and Alan, picked us up for the drive to Tampa. We had a pretty good inclination we wouldn't be returning to Sarasota for a long time.

I was doing okay. The waves of fear seemed to surface at the oddest times. I compiled a list of *positives* to keep with me to look at when I felt down. I had been blessed with such loving, supportive family members and friends whose emails, warm thoughts, and prayers were overwhelming.

There were times in my life I had thought I was special, but I never thought I would ever be *that* one in a million, with only three hundred chordoma cases in the United States a year. Being *special* in this way was something I certainly didn't want!

I turned to Chuck, who was reading but I suspect not concentrating very well, and said, "Do you realize I have something that is rarer than all the people who are in the Tampa airport right now, or even the entire population of Baltimore? That just absolutely blows my mind." He didn't reply. He just took my hand and gently brought it to his lips, then put his arm around my shoulder and pulled me closer to him.

Walking through the Johns Hopkins Outpatient Center for my appointment in the Meyer Building felt so different from the other times I had passed through these hallways as a patient, or as a volunteer for the Children's Center. It still looked the same, always reminding me of a waiting area at a train station, with black leather seats purposely arranged in waiting areas by departments. We walked past the information desk, pharmacy, vision center, and the Women's Board Café and Gift Shop. In the long tunnel to the main hospital we noticed the huge posters of yearly covers of *U.S. News and World Report* naming Johns Hopkins as the number one hospital in the country for nineteen consecutive years. Again, I felt very proud of my home city and this fabulous institution. Yet on that day I also felt a mix of emotions between anxiety and determination, fear and resolve. The elevator door opened on the seventh floor of Meyer, and we slowly walked towards the unknown with anxious uncertainty.

Chuck and I waited in a tiny, cramped office—not exactly what I would have expected for the Director of the Spine Center at Hopkins. Within minutes, a door opened, and a tall gentleman with a thick brown pompadour and moustache greeted us and ushered us into his office. This room was spacious, with a huge mahogany desk, matching bookcase, a teal blue sofa, several color coordinated comfortable chairs, and of course, the standard framed diplomas and awards adorning the walls.

After introducing himself and shaking our hands, Dr. Gokaslan told us he had reviewed the materials I sent him as well as all those that were faxed to the Spine Center from the Mayo Clinic. It surprised me when he asked what I knew about chordomas. I gave him an overview of what I learned from Dr. O'Connor, and what I had researched on the Spine Center and Chordoma Foundation websites. He thought I had been well-educated by Dr. O'Connor regarding the extent of the surgical procedure and the potential risks and problems associated with it. I told him that although we both believed she was an excellent physician, because of the rarity of chordomas, we didn't think Dr. O' Connor had enough surgical experience in this area. He said that the neurosurgeons at Hopkins perform two to three chordoma surgeries a month. I was really heartened to hear those statistics.

Dr. Gokaslan continued to explain that mine was a malignant tumor, which fortunately, as best as he could tell, was localized at the present time. He said the best treatment for this would be a complete resection of the tumor with negative margins and in an en bloc fashion. In other words, he recommended the complete removal of the tumor plus any diseased tissue or bone structure. This surgical procedure would require a multidisciplinary team including neurosurgeons, a plastic surgeon, a surgical oncologist, an orthopedist, and colon rectal and vascular surgeons if needed. Dr. Gokaslan proposed a posterior laminectomy, entering only from the back. Well, that certainly was a welcome piece of good news, and it differed significantly from the description of the surgical procedure we had received previously. *I'm so glad we had the presence of mind to seek a second opinion.*

While examining my back, Dr. Gokaslan asked me to bend over slightly. To my embarrassment, I passed gas during his exam. He assured me this was normal and was common with this diagnosis. I told him I had been having excessive, uncontrollable flatulence during the past year, and my internist said "most people pass gas about twenty-three times a day." I thought mine was much more than that. *Normally, this phenomenon goes undetected!*

Again we were told about the serious risks this surgical procedure had associated with it, including bleeding, infection, and paralysis with loss of bowel and bladder control, and a few others that I didn't want to think about. The risk of infection was very high with these surgeries, somewhere between thirty and forty percent. He went on to say that the surgery would be an all-day procedure requiring multiple teams, and I could expect to be in intensive care for several days. Then, barring complications, I would remain in the hospital for approximately two weeks. I also might require prolonged rehabilitation after surgery. He said there was a good probability that my bowel and bladder would not likely work for a period of time after surgery, even if the nerves were fully preserved.

My mind reeled. I was not thrilled about any of this, but I was ecstatic Dr. Gokaslan believed he could perform this complicated surgery by going in only from the back—sounded like a real plus, with the possibility of fewer complications. I was hoping that this wasn't just a pipedream.

After answering a few more questions Chuck had, Dr. Gokaslan told us he would like us to meet with Dr. Susan Gearhart, a colon rectal surgeon, so she could familiarize herself with my case in the event she is needed during my surgery. He said his secretary would set up the appointment for us.

"Is Dr. Gearhart related to Dr. John Gearhart, the pediatric urologist?" I asked.

"Susan is his wife," he responded.

"What a talented couple," I said.

Then Dr. Gokaslan asked us "the $64,000 question." Were we comfortable having the surgery here at Hopkins? Caught a bit off guard, I glanced over at Chuck, who said, "We want to move forward on this as quickly as possible. What are your thoughts, Sugah?"

"I guess I'm ready as I'll ever be."

Excusing himself while he made a phone call from his office, Dr. Gokaslan said he would be back shortly. I think we were both shocked when, after only a few minutes, he returned and told us that the surgery was scheduled for July 28, as long as everyone involved was available. *Wow! Only twelve days from today—I guess there's no turning back now.*

I asked him if he could give us a ballpark figure, or his best guesstimate as to what all of this was going to cost.

"Of course, each case is different, but it's in the thousands."

"So what are we talking about here?" I asked. "Are we talking about five thousand, or fifty thousand dollars?"

I could see he was uncomfortable with my question and was avoiding giving me a more definitive reply. He handed me a card and told us to go see Sandy, who was in charge of financial matters for neurosurgery in the Outpatient Center. We left his office, saying that we would be in touch.

Chuck thought we should go to lunch before we went to talk to the woman in Finances, but I just wanted to get this money thing resolved and move forward as quickly as possible. I had felt comfortable talking with Dr. Gokaslan and was very confident with him doing my surgery. What I didn't feel comfortable with was the financial piece of this puzzle, since he was only one of the many surgeons that would be involved with this intricate surgery.

We stopped at the Turtle Derby table in the Children's Center Hope Forest lobby as we made our way from the Meyer Building over to the Outpatient Center across the street. It was nostalgic for me to be there. How many years had I stood in this very space selling T-shirts, buttons, and turtle sponsorships as a fundraiser for the Child Life Department and the Perkins Day Care Center? Each year, as a prelude to the Maryland Preakness, the first-year medical and radiography students host this event and race sponsored turtles for the patients, their families, and staff in a picnic setting. Seeing the children's faces and hearing their squeals as they cheer for the turtles was priceless, and is one of my fondest memories as a Child Life volunteer.

Sandy was on the phone when we approached her desk unannounced, and signaled with her finger that she wouldn't be long. We waited in a nearby seating area until she called us back to her cubicle. I gave her a short version of the plan and asked her if she could give us a better estimate of what this surgery might cost. She was happy to help us and looked up the cost of the last one that was done recently, but forewarned us that she didn't know the exact circumstances or any of the details or particulars of this surgery. Whatever dollar figure she gave us would be a guess at best. For just the surgeon, the cost for the last similar procedure was approximately forty-eight thousand dollars. *Wow!*

Before either Chuck or I could respond, Sandy said, "Wait a second, I'm getting an email from Dr. Gokaslan as we speak. He is offering you a twenty percent discount." I had to laugh to myself, since Chuck always calls me the "Coupon Queen." Although I was happy with the discount, I did some quick calculations in my head and knew this concession would only represent a drop in the bucket, and the final cost of the surgery would still be a major financial hurdle for us.

Then came a massive shock; we were completely stunned when Sandy said, "You will have to pay the charge in full seven days prior to your surgery." The nightmare continued when she said, "Dr. Gokaslan doesn't accept any form of medical insurance."

Horrified, I said, "You have got to be kidding! How can average folks possibly pay for all of this up front?"

"Either with cash, a check, or a credit card."

Sandy saw the alarm on our faces and asked us if we would like to see Dr. Wolinsky, who accepts insurance. Simultaneously, we practically screamed YES! We recognized his name from our initial list of potential surgeons. After giving us his business card, she made a phone call and we were whisked off to his office in the Outpatient Clinic within ten minutes. Before we left, Sandy suggested that after talking with Dr. Wolinsky, we might want to stop by and talk with Peggy, their insurance resource specialist whose office was around the corner.

Our situation began to look better with this turn of events. Even though we were not sure who my lead surgeon would be, we at least felt confident I would be in the care of world-renown Johns Hopkins doctors.

After seeing the name Jean-Paul Wolinsky, M.D., on the card I had just stuck in my wallet, I walked into his office expecting to see someone wearing a beret, not cowboy boots. Rising from his chair, Dr. Wolinsky, a tall thin man with sandy hair, glasses and a warm smile, extended his hand to each of us and pointed to two chairs in the exam room. He told us he had just gotten off the phone with Dr. Gokaslan, who had briefed him about my case. I think we were surprised he already knew so much about me even before I had a chance to utter anything except, "Nice to meet you and thanks for seeing us without an appointment."

"I know more about you than you know about me," he said, "so I'll be happy to answer any of your questions or go over anything you need clarification on."

From our research we already knew Dr. Wolinsky was Associate Professor of Neurosurgery and Oncology, and his interests lay in neurosurgical oncology and complex spinal reconstruction. He received his medical degree from Baylor College of Medicine in Houston, Texas (which may have explained the cowboy boots), and also received specialized training in neurosurgical oncology at M.D. Anderson Cancer Hospital, also in Houston. After his neurosurgical residency, he completed an esteemed AOSpine fellowship in complex reconstructive spine surgery and spinal oncology at The Johns Hopkins Hospital.

After googling AOSpine, we had found that it is "an international community of spine surgeons, orthopaedic surgeons, neurosurgeons, academics, researchers, and other spine professionals," that provides "fellowships to budding spine surgeons with the opportunity to work in some of the world's top spine centers and learn from the best in the field." *Very impressive!*

Dr. Wolinsky methodically discussed my proposed surgery again with us, gave a similar analysis of the seriousness of my condition, and stressed the need to expedite the removal of the cancerous tumor. He explained his approach to this difficult and complicated procedure. He still wanted me to see Dr. Gearhart for a consultation.

"I usually like my patients to have proton beam radiation treatments at Massachusetts General in Boston sometime after they have completely healed from their surgery," Dr. Wolinsky said. "I will discuss this in more detail with you both during your follow-up appointments after being discharged. No need to think about this now. Do you have any further questions or concerns?"

"At Mayo, we were told the surgery would involve going in from the front *and* the back," I said. "We were just told that at Hopkins the surgery is performed by only going in from the back. Can you please explain this for us?"

"We used to operate both anteriorly and posteriorly, but we have found we have been more successful and have fewer complications by just going in posteriorly if we can." Listening to Dr. Wolinsky had a soothing effect on my anxiety. I felt more relaxed than I would have ever imagined. I think it was his calm, confident voice and gentle manner that I found so reassuring.

Then I asked him, "Are chordomas hereditary? I would hate to think that I could have passed this on to my two sons."

Dr. Wolinsky informed us that most people with a chordoma have no other family members with this type of cancer, but there are a very small number of families worldwide with multiple relatives who have chordomas. He didn't think I should concern myself with this at this time.

"I want to assure you that I accept most medical insurance," he told us. "I also want to let you know that if you are comfortable with me doing your surgery, I will be the lead surgeon and Dr. Gokaslan will assist. We team up on each other's surgeries—I assist on his and he assists on mine." That was music to my ears; like getting a "two-for-one." I felt like jumping off the chair and giving Dr. Wolinsky a big hug. This seemed like the best-case scenario ever and it took a huge burden off our shoulders. Without even consulting Chuck, I told Dr. Wolinsky I would like him to do my surgery.

4

The Focus

KEEPING MY EMOTIONS INTACT DURING the week and a half before my surgery was difficult to say the least. At times my mind wandered, straying back to the upcoming ordeal, I felt my body grow tense and my heart would begin to race. Closing my eyes, I tried to breathe deeply, concentrating only on my breath as I worked to block out all negative thoughts or worst-case scenarios. I was surprised how effective that simple exercise could be, and how grateful I had learned some breathing techniques in yoga class, and also from Dr. Andrew Weil's CD titled *Breathing*.

I wondered how my diagnosis, with all its uncertainty, was impacting Chuck. While many men have a difficult time openly expressing their thoughts and emotions, I am fortunate to have a partner who shares almost everything with me; whose love, encouragement, support and humor, are just a natural part of our marriage. I had always been attracted to Chuck's strong masculine side; his confidence, his resilience, his intelligence, his zest for learning, and the aura of strength he exuded. Yet, it was his softer side, his gentleness, his warmth, understanding, and sincerity that stole my heart. He is openly affectionate, the kind of man who dances with me in our kitchen in the middle of the day. I remember when I first introduced him at a family event to my Aunt Shirley, who was in her late eighties. She said, "It's about time we had a Southern gentleman in this family." (He's from Richmond, Virginia.)

But this situation—this crisis—was different. This was *cancer*, the big "C", the one that everyone fears, with mine being the one nobody (including many physicians) recognized or had ever heard of. Chuck's outward strength was reassuring, but I wondered what he was thinking inwardly; the thoughts he might not want to share, fearful he might upset me. I was concerned about the toll the stress might have on his health, since he has a long history of heart disease. Did he cry when I wasn't around? Did he confide in a friend or his family? Although we talked often, I hoped he had another outlet where he could vent and truly express himself.

The days passed quickly. We met with Dr. Susan Gearhart, a tall thin woman with a huge smile, whose cheerfulness and humor were certainly refreshing. She explained her role in this complex and difficult surgery. "I usually come in toward the end of the operation," she said. "Depending on what the team was able to accomplish, it is determined whether I need to take part in the actual surgery or just be there to check things out on my end. No pun intended!"

While she was examining me, she was also explaining things to a resident physician who was in the room with us. I never minded having residents or students being present during any of my appointments or procedures. This was Johns Hopkins, the leading teaching hospital affiliated with Johns Hopkins University School of Medicine, where the next generation of physicians and nurses were being trained. I never felt like a guinea pig. I was just happy someone could possibly learn something new or benefit from my case. I always felt it is a huge plus having such a vast pool of brilliant minds readily available for any medical discipline or "-ology" you could ever possibly need.

Dr. Gearhart wanted me to have a two-day prep before the surgery and gave me a sheet of instructions to follow. Glancing at the information, I could tell this was a lot more involved than a routine colonoscopy, which is everyone's favorite. Her last words before wishing me good luck were, "Take the enemas when they're offered; it will make things easier after the surgery." *Oh joy!*

Before leaving Hopkins, we stopped by Peggy's office, the insurance guru, just to make sure what our insurance would cover so there would be no surprises. Walking into her office was like being back in Sarasota—a tropical paradise with purple walls, a painting of two multi-colored toucans, a striped throw rug in hues of orange, red, lime, and teal, and a bouquet of similar colored artificial flowers adorning her desk. We knew right away we were going to like her. She was delightful, greeting us with a big smile and a warm welcome. Peggy sensed our nervousness right away and responded with concern couched in levity which soon had us in stitches. She sure lifted our spirits. When we finally got down to discussing our situation, Peggy was all business. Her knowledge was extensive, and as she answered our questions our anxieties began to melt away.

Guest Services, in the main lobby of the hospital, was our next stop. Although Chuck had received many invitations from family and friends to stay at their home while I was at Hopkins, we wanted to find out about other options the hospital might offer. He wanted to be closer to the hospital, and he didn't want to have to deal with the dreadful traffic on the Jones Falls Expressway twice each day. An accommodating staffer handed us brochures and information sheets with hotel discounts and descriptions of alternative housing around the Baltimore area, along with one describing The Hackerman-Patz Patient and Family Pavilion. She carefully explained the pros and cons of each option and said all would depend on availability. We expressed a possible interest in the Hackerman-Patz Pavilion, and she explained that we would have to apply and be approved to stay there. She told us we could apply through Joanne McMillian, the Housing Referral Coordinator, whose office was located in the Sidney Kimmel Comprehensive Cancer Center.

Over lunch, we decided the Hackerman-Patz Pavilion on Broadway and Orleans Streets on the hospital's campus would be the best option in our situation. The Pavilion was within easy walking distance to the hospital, which would mean we wouldn't have the added expense of renting a car. Designed specifically to provide housing for cancer patients and their caregivers, the Pavilion offered affordable accommodations in a home-like setting. It really sounded too good to be true.

Since my surgery was in one week, we were anxious to put in an application for the Pavilion. We didn't bother to walk over to see what it looked like first; we went straight over to talk with Joanne. She was just wonderful, having the perfect personality and patience for that job. After taking our application, she told us she would check on availability and would get back to us within a few days. I certainly hoped we were accepted and they had a room available. This would take a huge burden off our shoulders, and make it much easier on Chuck since he could go back to rest when he needed it.

Our last trip down to Johns Hopkins was for blood work. Convincing the lab technician to use a butterfly needle took some doing, but I told him even though the flow is slower, it would be easier on both of us, since lately I was a difficult "stick." With the blood work completed, Chuck and I walked over to the Hackerman-Patz Pavilion to see if we could tour the facility. We had received confirmation that we had been accepted. What a gift that was! We wouldn't realize until later just what a blessing this would turn out to be.

Chuck and I walked in unannounced to a lovely reception area and great room with a baby grand piano, flat screen television above the fireplace, and comfortable-looking group seating. Sarah was happy to take us on a tour. She explained they had both suites and apartment-style accommodations. On the first floor there was a library, a meditation room, and a multi-purpose family room. Taking the elevator to the second floor, we were shown a suite, which would provide a more affordable option for us. Each suite had a small living room with a recliner, loveseat, flat-screen TV, and telephone. Each kitchenette came equipped with a microwave, an apartment-sized refrigerator, sink, cabinets, coffee maker, table, and chairs. The bedroom had twin beds, a night stand with a telephone, a dresser with a mirror, and a nice-sized closet. The bathroom was equipped with a shower stall with a seat and adjustable shower head, and a hairdryer. Lest we forget for a moment we were not being shown summer vacation accommodations, we saw that hanging on the bathroom wall was a biohazards sharps disposal container. Sarah told us that all linens and towels would also be provided.

She then showed us a very large common area containing two fully-equipped kitchens. Each was furnished with basic appliances that were handicap accessible, and were stocked with every type of cookware, utensils, dishes, and glassware anyone could need. Also within this same common area was a large dining area furnished with several tables and chairs. We would have the choice of eating in our room, or having our meals in the dining area off the community kitchen. A laundry room was located near the kitchen/dining room area. Use of a washer and dryer was included at no additional cost, and high efficiency detergent was also provided. In the basement, there was a computer center, an activity room, and an integrated medical suite. There was free wireless Internet access throughout the building. *This just keeps getting better and better.* Whoever designed this facility was intimately aware of the special needs of cancer patients. It was designed by those who had thought of everything so people staying here wouldn't have to concern themselves with anything other than dealing with their major challenges.

After Sarah answered a few more questions, Chuck asked if she knew of a gym close by. We were told patients and caregivers who stayed there could use the gym in the Denton Cooley Center located on McElderry Street, a few blocks from the Pavilion. "I think the cost is fifteen dollars a week or thirty dollars a month," she said, "but I can verify that for you when we get upstairs." Having such well-planned and affordable housing within walking distance to Hopkins was really a dream come true for us. *Focus on the positive*, I told myself.

I received wonderful, supportive emails and notes from friends and family. So many people wanted to meet us for breakfast, lunch, dinner, coffee, or have us over. It would be impossible to visit with everyone, so we declined all the invitations. Chuck really wanted me to rest up before the surgery, and not be exhausted from running from pillar to post trying to see everyone. I knew all our friends and family had wonderful intentions, but I can honestly say I didn't have the emotional energy to support everyone else, trying to make them feel reassured. This was probably the first time in my life that I genuinely put *me* first.

We did do a few things that weren't medically related. Chuck insisted on taking me shopping for some "hospital-appropriate" nightgowns and a warm robe. We found a beautiful mint-colored terry robe in Nordstrom, several night shirts and gowns in T. J. Maxx, and a pair of slippers that I could easily slide my feet into. It was good to have little accomplishments at the end of the day, and to have the sense we were doing our best to think of everything (within our control) that could help me through the next few weeks.

Saturday, I attended services at my former synagogue in Baltimore, the one I had attended for over fifty years before moving to Sarasota. Although I always felt spiritually connected with God, I had a real need during this time to worship in the sanctuary where I grew up, where I became a Bat Mitzvah, where my sons had their Bar Mitzvah ceremonies, and where I shared so many wonderful memories with my father. A very real sense of peace surrounded me as I entered the synagogue. I felt so relaxed during the service, reciting and singing familiar prayers that were so much a part of me.

My thoughts drifted as a wave of nostalgia washed over me, accompanied with tears that I feverishly tried to keep at bay. I recalled past memories with astonishing clarity, memories of my father blessing the congregation, of the intense pride I felt for my two sons, Craig and Scott, as I placed their *tallitot* (prayer shawls) over their shoulders during their Bar Mitzvahs, and of the joy I felt as I watched them standing in front of the opened *Aron Kodesh* (ark) on Jewish holidays with their grandfather. These images came rushing in, overpowering my attempts to concentrate on the service. I searched for inspirational English readings in the *siddur* (prayer book) for comfort and a way to remove the odd feeling I had in the pit of my stomach. The reality of seeing my name listed under the *Refuah Shlema,* or healing prayer list, in our synagogue's weekly handout, was humbling.

Rabbi Adler's sermon was uplifting, filled with humor and thoughts to consider during the week. I realized how much I missed being here. I always loved it when he would leave the *bimah* (altar) to be with the congregation, to ask challenging, thought-provoking questions to make us think and learn. I silently said prayers for myself, Chuck, and my family. I prayed for my surgical team, asking God to please bless them with the knowledge and skill for a successful outcome. I realized how blessed I have been. I thought about staying to chat and catch up with people I had known for years after services, but I left as the closing song was being sung. Everyone meant well, but I didn't think I was mentally up for responding to everyone's questions and repeating the same answers over and over.

After finding out that Rabbi Adler would soon be going to Israel, I made a mental note to write a private message to give to him to place in the cracks of the Western or Wailing Wall (Kotel) in Jerusalem. This act of faith is a centuries-old tradition for Jews around the world. I figured I would need all the help and prayers

I could get. There was something calming about being able to take part in this time-honored practice from thousands of miles away, a way of confirming my faith in my intimately personal relationship with God.

We were fortunate to be able to move into the Pavilion the weekend before my surgery date. It gave us a chance to get settled and organized, fill the refrigerator and cabinets with food, and spend some quality time together, just the two of us without any family. Don't misunderstand, we enjoyed the time we had spent at our stepmom's condo the past week, and appreciated her "mothering" and everything she had done to make us feel at home. We just needed some space, some time alone, and some rest.

A quiet dinner at La Tavola in Little Italy was just what the doctor ordered. We knew it would be our last hurrah together for a long time and tried to be in the moment and not think about anything else. It was amazing how much I could eat, even though I still experienced waves of stomach tension that often rose throughout my day, my appetite never diminished.

After dinner, we walked arm-in-arm through the narrow streets of this charming, cozy neighborhood located in the heart of downtown Baltimore, nestled between the Inner Harbor and historic Fells Point. We topped off our evening by stopping for a delectable, lip-smacking Italian cannoli at Vaccaro's Italian Pastry.

On Sunday we met Bridget and Scott, Craig and Sonel, my brother, Dave and my nephew, Drew, for breakfast at the New Town Diner in Owings Mills. While everyone was ordering omelets or pancakes with hash browns and toast or bagels, I ordered hot tea and was "feasting" on the chicken broth and Jell-O I had brought with me, since my two-day liquid diet had already started. That breakfast together wasn't about the meal—it was about surrounding myself with the people who were most important in my life, the ones who I loved dearly and who brought me the most joy. It was Dave's birthday and we celebrated with a cake I brought for the occasion, even though, when we spoke on the phone, he had told me not to do anything because "tomorrow is all about you, not about me."

I handed Craig and Scott a sealed note I had written to them as we left the restaurant. Craig and Sonel followed us back to the Pavilion so we could give them back their car which they had let us borrow ever since we arrived in Baltimore. We showed them our suite and they gave Chuck a little gift, a one pound bar of Trader's Joe's dark chocolate. *How sweet it is!*

July 26

Dear Family and Friends,

You have no idea how much your expressions of concern, warm emails, and prayers mean to both Chuck and me. We are blessed with a wonderful support group of family and friends who are helping make this difficult journey so much easier.

My surgery is scheduled for July 28, and I will be in ICU for one to two days, and will be confined to bed for three to five. If all goes well, I'll be at Hopkins for two weeks and probably have rehab and then another week before I can return to Sarasota. Their goal is to remove the tumor intact without damaging any of the sacral nerves involved, causing problems with the bladder and bowel. They will go in from the back only, and it will be an all-day operation.

Chuck was approved for housing at the Hackerman-Patz Pavilion, a block from the hospital. It was designed specifically for cancer patients, and has a suite with a small living room, nice-sized bedroom, bathroom, kitchenette, Internet access, a gym close by, shuttles, etc. So he won't need a car, and can exercise and go back and forth to visit. Their daily rate is reasonable. This is a huge weight off our shoulders. We will be moving in this Friday for some R&R before my prep.

A card or note would be greatly appreciated. If you insist on doing anything else (no flowers, hospital rule), I hope you will consider making a donation to the: Alzheimer's Association, Florida Gulf Coast Chapter, 3277A Fruitville Road, Suite 1, Sarasota, FL, 34237. This chapter has made a huge difference in the lives of so many people.

Chuck will be sending updates after July 28th, and will let you know when I'm up for visitors.

Thanks again.

With love,

Susan

5

No Turning Back

IT WAS EERIE NOT SEEING any people on Broadway when Chuck and I walked from the Pavilion to the hospital at 5:10 in the morning on Tuesday. I was at peace. Getting up early to recite the prayers I had brought with me provided an aura of tranquility. I had done the best possible prep the night before—now things were out of my control and in the hands of God and my surgeons. I left a note for Chuck on the bed back at the Pavilion. Words didn't come easily, my thoughts interrupted by images of the special memories we've shared. In my mind the note had to be just right, but in reality I knew he would be moved by anything I wrote. Being confident this wasn't the last card I would ever give to him, I wanted it to be a tribute to the love and bond which we are blessed with.

We walked through the iron gates which lead to a circular driveway draped in well-manicured hues of lavender, rose, and white flowers. We entered through the door of the center building and former entrance, one of the three remaining original buildings which opened in 1889. This four-story building now houses the Billings Administration Offices, with an open rotunda, an octagonal design, and exquisite mahogany paneling and intricate woodwork.

Chuck paused at the ten-and-a-half-foot marble statue of Jesus Christ, which rises beneath its historic dome. Tears welled as I watched him bow his head in prayer. Standing to the side, I recalled the times when I had seen young children—some with bald heads, some in wheelchairs, some toting IV poles—standing before this enormous sculpture, eyes lifted towards a face that brought much solace to so many during extraordinarily difficult times. At that moment, I had dramatic images of people touching the pierced foot of this iconic figure, so many that the marble is worn smooth, or placing flowers on the pedestal inscribed with a quote from Saint Matthew's Gospel: "Come unto me all ye that are weary and heavy laden and I will give you rest."

The Meyer Building was easy to find. I had walked these halls so many times, maneuvering from building to building was "old hat." We patiently waited for instructions in a small sitting area on the seventh floor. Finally, someone came to escort me back to wherever, telling Chuck he would be able to come back after I had been prepped. I gave him a quick kiss on the cheek, and followed this unidentified woman back to a small room with wooden cabinets and a single bed. I was instructed to put on the gown that was lying on the bed, and she would return shortly. (I find it annoying when people address you by your name, but think it's not important to reciprocate with theirs. I believe this simple courtesy of telling patients your name should be reinforced in "Intro to Patient Care 101" in all fields of medicine.)

With all my clothes neatly tucked away in a plastic drawstring bag, I attempted to focus on recalling the list of positive affirmations that were in my wallet back at the Pavilion, rather than looking at the clock as the time slowly ticked away. I knew Craig and Dave were coming before the surgery, and Buddy was on his way from Richmond to be with his Dad. Scott said he'd be here as soon as his presentation at work was finished later that morning. It was comforting to think of my loved ones, as I was sure they were also thinking of me.

Another woman who also didn't identify herself came in the room and asked if I was able to walk or did I need a wheelchair? I followed her to a large room with many beds that were separated by light blue and green striped curtains. Up I went onto another gurney, and there I stayed and waited for someone to come in, which in my mind was more than a half an hour. Finally I sat up and pulled back the curtain as best I could and said in a boisterous voice, "Does anyone remember I'm back here?" A man and a woman dressed in scrubs turned and said, "The nurses just arrived, so it won't be too much longer." *What? Why did we have to get here at 5:30 if the nurses don't arrive until 6:30? Calm yourself, Susan. Getting yourself aggravated won't make things move any faster.* I was just anxious to see Chuck and my family, and I saw no reason why they couldn't have been with me all this time.

It wasn't too long before a middle-aged woman came in to put in my IV. She had difficulty finding a good vein and eventually stuck me near my wrist. After fishing, she said, "I got it."

"No, you don't," I said, and calmly asked her to remove the needle. I had enough experiences in hospitals to know she had blown a vein. Her second try wasn't much better, and I requested that someone else attempt to get this IV started. Agreeably enough, she left and sent in a young man who introduced himself as "Jason." Jason was animated and a real comedian. Within minutes he had the IV in and flowing properly. As he taped my wrist that was now throbbing, I said, "I wish they had sent you in first."

Before I knew it, Chuck, Craig, and Dave were at my side. All smiles and upbeat, they brought up things that would make me smile and laugh. I think all of us were trying to hold it together for each other. I asked Chuck to come closer. With a girlish grin I asked, "You won't forget to bring the tweezers?" Amused, he said, "I'll remember." (We had made a pact that if I was ever in a nursing home, he would bring tweezers and pluck those annoying little black chin hairs that seem to surface with age.)

Things moved quickly, and a young woman from anesthesia came to give me the low-down on what to expect. She said I didn't have to be concerned about the bowel prep being adequate enough for this type of surgery, since I would be getting an enema in the operating room after I was asleep. *Hooray!* To know I'd be asleep when they gave me the enema was a blessing. Pity the poor soul that has that responsibility.

"It's time," she said. I turned to kiss Craig and Dave, and did my best to look cheery as Chuck bent over to give me a big hug. I didn't want to let go, but knew if I prolonged this farewell any longer, I might not be able to hold it together. Up went the side rails. "See all of you guys later," I said as I threw them each a kiss. "Love you." I closed my eyes and said my last prayer on the way to the operating room. That's all I remember.

6

Can Anybody Hear Me?

I HEARD CHUCK'S VOICE CALLING "SUGAH." Who could miss his cute Southern accent? I couldn't see him. I realized that I was on my stomach. I felt woozy. I could hear someone talking but it sounded muffled to me. I couldn't make out exactly what they were saying. I was conscious enough to notice that my left wrist was hurting, probably from the two unsuccessful attempts to get an IV started. I could tell the top of my face was on a pillow, but my nose and mouth were in some sort of open space. I was conscious of a blood pressure cuff on my right arm and an oxygen gizmo on my finger. I was cold.

I felt someone touch my shoulder, then a breath close to my neck. I heard Chuck's voice. "Sugah, the operation is over. You did great! Dr. Wolinsky was able to remove the tumor intact. He was also able to preserve the S2 and S3 nerves." I couldn't respond. I felt tightness in my throat and tears moistening my cheeks. It was difficult to swallow. My eyes were closed as I silently recited the *Shema*, in Hebrew, *Hear, O Israel: The Lord is our God, the Lord is one.* I was so, so grateful!

Finally, I turned my head to the left and saw my wonderful husband bending down to be at my level. "Darling," I said, "Are you sure he got it all?"

"That's definitely what Dr. Wolinsky said. It truly is a miracle," he whispered.

"Where am I?"

"In the NCCU [Neuro Critical Care Unit]."

"What time is it?"

"It's about eight o'clock at night. Your children are in the waiting room and want to see you. Is it all right for them to come in?"

I knew I was falling asleep, but I wanted to see my children. I managed to keep my head turned to the left just enough to see four midriffs in navy blue, white with blue stripes, purple, and pink crowded together. I couldn't lift my head to see their faces, but I would know those voices anywhere. "Mom, you did great!" "You were a champ!" "You're going to be okay." My cheerleaders all seemed to be talking at the same time.

"Love you all," I managed to say as I was beginning to drift off. I slowly turned my head back to a more tolerable position. Chuck (I guess it was Chuck) kissed me on the back of my head and said, "Get some......"

As my eyes were closing, my thoughts were muddled. Occasionally I heard voices and conversation but they were muted. If they were directed towards me, I didn't respond. As I listened to the rhythmic beep of what I guessed was a monitor, I had this crazy idea to try to remember everyone's telephone numbers. I had read somewhere that anesthesia can temporarily affect your memory, and I knew I had had an all-day procedure. Down the list I went; first the kids, then a few friends, never knowing if they were really correct, but accurate enough to satisfy me that my recall was still working. Feeling extremely drowsy, I rattled off numbers, 410-653...

Slowly I attempted to open my eyes, with little success. Blinking in confusion, I took time to try to figure out where I was. I was quite sure I was still on my stomach, my forehead rested on a pillow and the rest of my face in some sort of open space. My shoulders ached. My arms felt like lead weights, and I was sure a pile of books rested on my butt. My mouth was parched. I was conscious my left wrist was still throbbing.

Then I heard voices in the distance. I had no idea what day or time it was. *What do you do now, Susan?* This is so unlike me but I shouted, "Hello, hello, is anyone here?" I didn't know what else to do and I needed to get someone's attention.

It was so wonderful to hear that familiar Southern drawl. "I'm here, Sugah. I've been here since your surgery."

"Am I still in intensive care?"

"Talk louder, I can hardly understand you," Chuck said as he stroked my hair.

"Am I still in intensive care?" I yelled again.

"No, you're in your own private room now," Chuck replied.

"What day is it?" I asked. *This is crazy. My mouth is so dry my tongue is stuck to my palate. I can hardly talk with this mattress pressing on my throat.* I wasn't aware that with my head down my words were directed to the floor, making it difficult to understand what I was saying. *Who cares what day it is?*

I struggled, trying to draw enough air into my lungs to make my voice heard.

I tried again. "WATER!"

"I'll go ask the nurse what you're allowed to have," Chuck whispered. *Thank goodness he heard and understood me.*

Drifting in and out of wakefulness, I felt a hand on my shoulder. "Sugah, here are some ice chips. Can you turn your head to the left for me?" he asked. Weak and weary, conscious of the dull ache in my neck, I slowly turned towards Chuck's voice. I tried to slurp up the pieces of ice Chuck was trying to spoon-feed me, realizing many were hitting the floor. The melting coolness felt amazing, as I savored every chip that made it into my mouth. Turning my head back down to be more comfortable, also made it more difficult for Chuck to feed me ice chips, and more hit the floor.

All during this time my arms were outstretched by my side. Still very tired and hoping to ease the pain, I slowly moved my arms above my head to rest on a pillow. Exhausted, I drifted back to sleep.

July 29

Dear Family and Friends,

Susan has been moved from NCCU (Neurosciences Critical Care Unit) to a regular room on the 8th floor of the Meyer Building. I worked with her nurses to jerry-rig her bed, trying to transform it into what would be similar to the bed she had while in NCCU, comparable to a massage table which has a hole for your face and a padded area for your forehead. I built a platform literally from the ground up, by stacking glove boxes on top of each other and adding pillows so she could rest her forehead on the pillow to be more comfortable. She will probably remain on her stomach at least until tomorrow night.

She is doing well, although she is still in a lot of pain and requires medication. Her blood pressure and blood sugar are good. She is resting better. Her face is still quite puffy and her lips are huge. Dr. Wolinsky talked to both of us this evening and reemphasized that they believe they got it all and that she should eventually recover with normal bowel and bladder function. Praise God! Not sure how much of this Susan is going to remember, since she continues to fade in and out. She sends everyone her love. Please continue to pray for us. No flowers please.

Chuck

7

This Is Not Working!

M Y DAYS AND NIGHTS WERE running together. I had lost all sense of time. Lying on my stomach put me at a definite disadvantage when various staff came in to work and talk with me. Using only the sound of their voices, I conjured up images of what doctors, nurses, techs, and housekeeping staff looked like. Their gender was easy, but other details became a game for those times when I was fully awake. Thank goodness everyone identified themselves and explained what function they were doing. I could hardly wait to turn over to see the people who were caring for me.

Memories of my detached retina surgery at Hopkins Wilmer Eye Institute in 1977 surfaced. That surgery was a week after my first son, Craig was born. Back then I was on my back, but was bilaterally patched for two weeks, couldn't see a thing, and had to rely on my other senses to compensate. I remember wondering if it was worse to be born with sight and lose it, or never to have any sight at all? I decided that the latter would be worse. Being born blind, you wouldn't know what a horse or anything actually looked like; whereas if you had sight and lost it, your mind would still maintain vivid images of how things looked from your memory bank and past experiences. Even though I couldn't see the TV, I had known what our local anchors looked like and I was familiar with their voices. I was glad to know the patches were temporary, and that I had 20-20 vision in my other eye.

Now, two women from occupational therapy came in to help me. They adjusted things on my bed to make me more comfortable. I heard them talking to Chuck and to someone I thought might be my nurse, but I really didn't understand all that they said. "We're going to move you higher," they told me, "and if you can help us that would be great." Evidently there was a person on each side of my bed, because the next thing I felt were hands under my armpits moving me forward as my chin brushed against the rough sheets. "Is this better for you?" one of them asked. They didn't hear my muffled, "NO!" Before I could yell again, they placed what felt like a long piece of hard foam under my chin. *Great, before I was just sore from a scraped chin. Now I feel like I can't swallow. These therapy people sound sweet—I know they're trying their best to find ways to help me, but THIS IS NOT WORKING—it's worse!*

As soon as I thought occupational therapy had left, I pulled the hard foam away and dropped it on the floor. "**This is not working!**" I screamed.

Later, when I was awake enough to think clearly, I wondered why Hopkins—who supposedly did more chordoma surgeries than most—didn't have a special bed for patients who had to lie on their stomachs for long periods of time. *Is this any way to run an airline?*

July 30

Hey All,

It has been a grueling night and day. Susan remains on her stomach and this is incredibly uncomfortable for her. The doctors tell me her face is very puffy from the position she was in during her long surgery and from being on her stomach for so long. I worked with occupational therapy this afternoon trying to make her more comfortable. Hopefully, they will be able to turn her onto her side tomorrow afternoon or early evening. That's the plan anyway. Dr. Wolinsky told me plastic surgery makes the call on when she can turn over and lay on her side. He said Susan was his first patient ever positioned on their stomach after chordoma surgery. Her vitals remain good.

I had approximately 2 hours sleep last night while staying with Susan. This afternoon I asked Craig to relieve me and I went home to the Pavilion and crashed for 3 hours. I'm back at the hospital now on Craig's computer typing this.

That's it for now. Please keep us in your prayers. We send you our love.

Chuck

Lying on my stomach was getting really old. Chuck told me I had been positioned like this for three days. It seemed more like ten to me. I kept alternating between putting both arms by my side or raising them up and folding them under my chin, neither of which was too pleasant. After my back surgery in 1971, I could never sleep on my stomach. When I tried, it had felt like my back locked which made it much harder to turn over. This time was much worse; I was truly miserable.

They kept telling me I would be turned over soon, but "SOON" wasn't coming fast enough. I had known I'd be in bed for three to five days after my operation, which I thought was contrary to what the norm was after surgery—but no one ever mentioned I would have to lie on my stomach the entire time. *Patience, Susan. This is a small price to pay for the gift of life.*

The historic moment finally came, although I wasn't sure what day or time it actually happened. After sliding me downward so my head was back on the bed, the nurses instructed me to roll my entire body over, all at once, making sure not to lift my upper torso and legs off the bed. They helped me roll on to my right shoulder as their hands guided me until I was able to place my right hand on the side rail and slowly leaned against the pillows that were propped along my back. *AT LAST THIS ORDEAL IS OVER!* I breathed a big sigh of relief. It probably only took a few minutes, but it seemed like forever. I'm so glad my biggest fan and cheerleader was there to witness this small but significant step towards my road to recovery.

"What am I lying on?" I asked, now that I could see who I had been speaking to.

"You have two drains coming out of your butt," one nurse replied. "We'll just pin your grenades to the front of your gown with a safety pin." My nurse explained the drains were used to insure the surgical site does not collect the extra fluid the body normally produces after an operation. She told me someone would empty them a few times each day. *Another little tidbit they neglected to tell me. They look more like Christmas ornaments. So glad I'm in a hospital gown.*

July 31

Hi All,
After another night of discomfort from lying on her stomach, Susan greeted me by saying, "You were snoring last night." I knew right then and there that we had turned another corner and she was making progress!
What a great day for us!!!!!!!!! At 6 AM, one of the neurosurgical residents told me they would turn Susan onto her side sometime near noon. I made sure that he understood that she could not lie comfortably on her left side. He also said that she could begin a liquid diet.
At 6:30 AM I explained to the nurse that Susan normally followed a specific daily regimen at home to help with bowel movements – Citracel in the morning along with her Wonder Mixture of All Bran, applesauce, and prune juice. Sometime during her day she ate a handful of prunes.
At 10 AM I went home to eat breakfast, get cleaned up, and grab a nap. I was back at the hospital at 11:55 AM. Susan was still on her stomach, so I asked the nurse when she would be turned to her side. She said that she had already paged a physician assistant and the turn should be within the hour. Another resident came by expecting to see Susan already

moved. He checked her out and said she was doing very well and that her swelling would improve once she was turned over.

Susan's current bed was a mess, with pads, towels, pillows and sheets and blanket askew. The more I looked at it, the more I thought that trying to put new linens on that bed while Susan was still in it was going to be difficult at best and very uncomfortable for her. So I suggested that we prepare a new bed with linens and move Susan from the old bed to it. The nurses agreed and we completed the transfer at 1:30 PM. I say "we" completed it, but really, it was Susan who performed the lion's share. She scooted from the old bed to the new with our help and once on the new bed, using the side rails she positioned herself so the nurses could place supporting pillows where needed. She is truly one amazing woman. Once turned, I swear you could almost see her swollen lips and eyes begin to improve. I placed drops in her eyes and applied Vaseline to her lips and chin which had been scraped on a rough sheet.

Shirley (her stepmom) called me on my cell phone. After a brief conversation with her I handed the phone to Susan. Together they sang the prayer for lighting the Sabbath candles, a tradition Susan has been doing most of her life. I could tell Susan was truly moved by Shirley's thoughtfulness and this special connection they had shared between them.

Susan had me place the wonderful cards she has begun receiving on a shelf by the window where she can enjoy them from her bed. She instructed me that I was not to spend tonight at the hospital and by the time she "shooed" me out, around 10 PM, she was drinking liquids, inserting eye drops and putting Vaseline on her lips and chin by herself. She gave me specific instructions as to what I am to bring to her tomorrow. She told me her nurse said they might try to get her up the next day. Her spirits are really high.

All in all, this has been a great day for both of us and we so much appreciate the wonderful support we have received. Thanks everyone from the bottom of our hearts.

Love,

Chuck

8

I'm Not Oriental

THERE WAS A KNOCK AT the door. "Housekeeping," a woman's voice announced. This short, buxom lady in a blue uniform began mopping the floor. She turned to me and said, "If you don't mind me asking, are you the same lady that's been in this room the past couple of days?"

"I haven't been too with-it lately," I replied, "but I think I'm one and the same."

"Honey, your face and eyes were so puffy; I thought you were Oriental," she said with a smile. "You don't look like the same person."

"No, I'm not Oriental; actually I'm Jewish." That just cracked her up, and we laughed together until I realized how much my laughter was increasing the pain. *I can't wait to share this one with Chuck.*

How comforting it was to see Chuck walk in each morning, always with a smile, with his orange and grey backpack filled with items I needed, his book to read, and the emails he had printed out from friends and family. His morning hello kiss was such a refreshing start to my day. Although the swelling gradually subsided, I still was in a considerable amount of pain. The bandage on my back was cumbersome, although it had been changed a couple of times by a nurse from Wound Care. The drains were more than annoying, and had to be emptied several times a day.

The word came down from the powers-that-be that I could begin to have solid food. *Hooray!* I have a hefty appetite for a relatively thin woman and really have to be sick to not eat. My mother always said when I was younger, "When you stop eating, I'm taking you straight to the hospital." It's not much different now.

How nice it was to be handed my first daily menu by a young man dressed in black slacks, a long-sleeved white shirt, and a tuxedo style bow tie. I so looked forward to his visits. Even with his five-star-hotel appearance, I still knew I was in a hospital, but this almost-elegant service was a nice touch. Chuck methodically went through the options for each meal and circled my selections for me. I was still pretty weak.

Despite getting pain meds and something to help me sleep, nights were still difficult. I was taught the proper way to turn by rolling my whole body at once. Not having much strength made turning a major event. My hospital gown would often get tangled underneath me, or I'd be lying on one of the drains, and just couldn't get comfortable. Even in a semi-conscious sleep, I was aware of my blood pressure being taken during the night. It seemed whenever I was finally in a good REM sleep, a parade of neurosurgical residents would come in around 6:30 AM to check my incision, or the hematologist would need way too much of my blood. *I am so tired. I am so, so tired.*

August 1

Hey all!

Susan continues to make progress each day. Today she began eating a regular diet. She said she had "institutional" eggs for breakfast—yummy. She ordered a pizza and prunes for supper and ate the prunes and about a third of a slice of the personal size pizza. Guess who ate the rest. It really WAS very good.

She is doing most personal things for herself – brushing her teeth, drinking liquids, etc.

They were supposed to get her up today, but it had to be postponed when she told the nurse that she was experiencing pains in her right leg – near the front of her shin. As a precaution, they will perform an ultrasound test to make sure there are no blood clots. None are suspected.

Only her children and her brother, Dave have visited, and only for short periods. Susan is so happy to see them, but she tires easily. Dave brought her a very neat picture he had taken of all of us when we had breakfast two days before her surgery at the New Town Diner. He had it blown up to about 12 X 24 inches. I hung it above her wipe-off board. She loves telling everyone about her family.

I was asked to send out the address where friends and family could send cards.

You're the best!

Chuck

One morning, two very upbeat nurses showed me the best way to get out of bed more comfortably. With the head of my bed raised, they helped me use my arms and hands to push myself up, and gingerly moved both my legs together until they dangled on the side of the bed. Placing the walker in front of me, they waited until I was ready to try to stand. With my hands positioned firmly on the walker, I leaned forward, pressing down with my hands as I slowly rose to an upright position. Did it feel wonderful! My legs felt like rubber bands, but it was great to stand up. Continuing to put my weight on my hands, I slowly took a few steps. With the encouragement of Chuck, my favorite advocate, and with two nurses by my side, I walked towards the door of my room.

"Can I walk in the hallway?" I asked.

"We'll walk with you to make sure you're steady and your balance is okay," they said. "Before you go in the hallway, we need to hook your urine drainage bag to your walker. It might be a good idea to put a robe on," one nurse said jokingly. I was so excited to be out of bed, I had not thought about putting on a robe. Modesty is not the priority when you're in a hospital, and you really need help from so many people. Everyone had been fantastic and I felt so grateful for their help.

I caught a glimpse of myself in the mirror as I passed the bathroom. My face looked pale and very puffy. Chuck and both nurses assured me that what I saw was a huge improvement over what I had looked like. Chuck said, "When you were on your stomach, Sugah, your lips were huge and you were drooling a lot." *Don't remember any of that which probably is a good thing. Susan, you need to concentrate on putting one foot in front of the other for now.* It was so wonderful to be out of bed and moving again, even if at a snail's pace. With each step it felt like I had a "fanny pack" filled with rocks on my butt. Wearing a mint-colored robe, white surgical stockings, and blue footies, I was just a vision of loveliness! *Oh well, I'm on my way!*

Simultaneously, Chuck and I noticed the large framed print hanging on the wall through the open doorway in an office directly across from my room. It was a picture of an open window with a sheer white and blue striped curtain blowing in the wind, the exact same one Dr. Holt, my Baltimore rheumatologist, has hanging in his waiting room. What a coincidence. Dr. Holt was instrumental in sending me to the Mayo Clinic. Am I ever grateful!

Later that afternoon, Chuck walked with me down the hall and back. I was more sure of myself. The last thing I wanted to do was fall. We paused in front of a bulletin board to look at the pictures of chordomas and sacretomy operations and read the explanations. Dr. Wolinsky saw us and asked how I was doing. "Not bad," I replied. "I'm not exactly ready for a marathon, but delighted I'm up."

"We're pleased also," he said. "None of my patients has ever been placed on their stomach for so long after surgery. It's 'Plastics' call concerning patient placement. I know you were miserable."

"Since you were able to remove my chordoma intact, am I cancer-free now?"

Dr. Wolinsky answered, "I wouldn't go that far and say you are cancer-free. Remember I told you chordomas tend to grow back, and that's why we will have to continually monitor you for many years. Just concentrate on getting your strength back and we'll talk more later."

August 2

Hi Everybody,

Well today was a very good day for us. I thought when PT finally arrived this afternoon, Susan would be allowed to get up and sit in her chair. Was I surprised! Susan got out of the bed by herself and then, using a walker proceeded to walk with two nurses around the entire floor and then walk down a long hallway to the exit and back. Later on, she did it again with just me. Praise GOD!!!

She had pizza again today for lunch. For dinner, she had tuna salad with grapes, half a wheat roll, tomato basil soup, red Jell-O, vanilla ice cream, and a cup of hot tea.

I had a tuna fish sandwich.

Please keep up the prayers, they are obviously working!

Chuck

August 3

Hi All,

I think I was a little too optimistic in my last email. Susan's struggle continues. Today she was very uncomfortable and tired. She was evaluated by teams from OT, PT, Dermatology, Wound Care, and Rehab. The wonderful news today is she walked without a walker for the first time. She still will need to use a walker sometimes, but as her strength returns she will need it less and less. She certainly has not lost her appetite. I saw her lunch and dinner trays and they looked like "Sherman marching across Georgia." Wasn't much left!!

The game plan is to remain on this floor for a few more days, as determined by her neurosurgical team and then move her to another floor for rehab. We don't know now how long she will have to remain in the hospital, but we do know that she will have to remain in Baltimore for at least one week after she is released.

She loves the get-well cards, emails (I copy some of them each day for her), and the prayers she knows are being said on our behalf. It truly is a blessing to have such wonderful relatives and friends.

Chuck

9

On to Rehab

L YING ON MY SIDE, FACING the window, I heard the now familiar shuffle of footsteps entering my room. Without glancing at my watch, I knew it was somewhere between six and six-thirty in the morning, the usual time when the neurosurgery and/or plastic surgery teams made their rounds. You have to love these guys. I learned to stay put and let them come around to face me rather then turning over to accommodate them, avoiding added pain which came with turning onto my side. They usually asked how I was feeling, how's my pain, and politely asked if they could look at my incision.

"Looks good," the head doctor commented, as the rest of the pack headed for the door. Actually, from what I gathered from the comments of other doctors, nurses, and staff who saw my incision, Dr. Simmons (my plastic surgeon) had done an excellent job putting me back together. One nurse told me, "This is beautiful—and I've seen some that really aren't."

I was really sorry I had mentioned that something on my upper left leg was annoying me with an itchy and a slightly burning sensation. Before I could blink, there was a flurry of activity and staff was running in and out of my room. Dermatology was called, two doctors evaluated the site, a biopsy was taken, and just in case it was contagious, a special protocol was set up outside my room. From that point on, everyone who entered my room had to don a yellow gown, then rubber gloves, mask and shoe covers.

I apologized to most folks, somewhat embarrassed by the trouble I was causing them. At the same time it was comical to see how the "one-size-fits-all" gown looked on the various body shapes and heights of the staff. As I watched each person who entered stuff their gown and accessories in a large hamper as they left my room, my concern heightened for what effect this would have on our environment.

Chuck had gone to the gym early so he could be there when I was moved to the Comprehensive Inpatient Rehabilitation Unit on the third floor of the Halsted Building. Dr. Wolinsky was thrilled I had been accepted. Not all his patients had been so fortunate, since the rehab unit only has fourteen beds.

Shortly following our daily after-breakfast stroll, Dr. Michelle Clarke, a Neurosurgery AOSpine fellow, came into my room to let me know she would be completing my paperwork for my discharge from neurosurgery and transfer to rehab. "Don't get too excited," she said, "Things often don't move as quickly as we would like around here. A nurse will be in to go over your discharge instructions with you and your husband. Just in case I don't get back before you leave, I'll say goodbye now and wish you the best of luck with your recovery. You have made great progress, but you have a long way to go. Keep up the good work in rehab."

I liked Dr. Clarke. She was delightful to talk to and so down to earth. (Not pompous like many doctors who think they are God's gift to medicine.) It wasn't until I was fully conscious after my surgery that I found out she had assisted at my operation. What a great team I had!

With the paperwork completed and instructions given, I took another walk down to the nurses' station to thank everyone who had helped with my recovery. Transport was waiting for me when I returned, making sure I was comfortable and secure in their wheelchair, carefully placing my urine bag next to me. Chuck piled a few light items on my lap and put the rest of my personal belongings in the small suitcase he had brought.

"Ready, Sugah?" he asked.

"Most definitely," I said, looking up at him but not commenting on the teary look I saw in his eyes. This was a great moment for us. I was still in a lot of pain; the catheter was getting more and more irritating, but I was looking forward to the next step on my journey.

My rehab room was at the end of a long hallway. Surprisingly, it was huge and came equipped with a bathroom I hoped I would be using some time soon. I had a great view of the stunning red brick wall of another building.

A nurse in lavender scrubs introduced herself and began taking vitals and explaining what to expect while I was in rehab. She was interrupted when Dr. Robert Mayer, Medical Director of Inpatient Rehabilitation, and Dr. Nathan Neufeld, Chief Resident, came in to talk to me about their goals and expectations for my recovery. They had outlined the Acute Inpatient Rehabilitation Program that I would be participating in. I would be working with a physical therapist for gait, balance, transfers, endurance, and strength. An occupational therapist would help me with activities of daily living, while nurses would deal with the neurogenic bowel and bladder issues that resulted from of my extensive surgery, along with wound care.

Dr. Mayer told us we would meet my team later that day and they would then explain the routine I would be following while in rehab. "It's an intense program, but we've had great success with it. A lot of that success comes from the patient and their willingness to put into action what they learn in PT and OT." *Take a deep breath Susan.* All of this seemed like it was a bit too soon. I walked like a sumo wrestler, could only tilt my head forward, tired easily, and despite the meds, was still in intense pain. *Don't panic girl, until you hear what the team expects.*

When we arrived, the women in the family room stood and introduced themselves as my physical and occupational therapists. Chuck helped as I gingerly lowered myself to a comfortable couch and then sat beside me. They handed me a notebook and suggested I browse through it at my leisure when I returned to my room. They recommended I make a list of any questions I may have for them when I began therapy the next day. "We try our best to keep to the scheduled daily routine, with one and half hours of PT in the morning and about the same of OT in the afternoon. We have designed this schedule specifically for your medical needs," said Stacey, "but we can make adjustments as needed."

By the time Chuck walked me back to my room, I was exhausted and decided this notebook could wait until I was better able to focus on its content. I encouraged Chuck to go back to the Pavilion to get some rest. My eyes were closing as he kissed me goodbye. I whispered I would call him later. That's all I remember until I woke up and saw my dinner tray sitting beside my bed.

August 5

Hey Everybody,

Today was a very good day for us. Susan still suffers pain and discomfort, but today it was not as bad as yesterday. I guess that cliché "Time heals all...." is true.

Susan was moved to Rehabilitation on a new floor this morning and the change seems to have really made her feel better. She still has a private room with her own private bath. The room is quite large and she has a striking view of the back wall of another building with its air conditioning exhausts. Red brick must have been in vogue at Hopkins for the last 100 years or so.

I need to share an experience with you. Susan was standing at the sink in her bathroom in her old room. She was in the buff. I was standing right behind her in case she felt weak. The bathroom door was open. There was a knock on the door and I said "Come in." Susan yelled, "No, tell them to wait!" When she was all back together, I opened the door to the room and there stood the Jewish chaplain for Hopkins. Now you have to picture this. This rabbi is a very large man. Because Susan was in isolation, he had to put on this dumb looking yellow robe thingy which ties in the back and also had to don a pair of purple rubber gloves. There he stood with the arms of the robe only reaching up to his elbows and the top of the robe reaching just above his bellybutton. It was a real Kodak moment. Susan and I both could hardly keep from laughing ourselves silly.

Susan just called me and gave me her schedule of activities tomorrow:

> *7:30-8:30 breakfast*
>
> *10:30-12:00 physical therapy*
>
> *12:30-1:30 lunch*
>
> *2:00-3:30 occupational therapy*
>
> *5:30-6:30 dinner*

I plan to be with her all day.

Craig and Dave came to visit this evening and Dave brought Susan a notebook computer to use as soon as she is up to it. Her backlog of messages is enormous. Her appetite remains very good. Her lunch was delayed today because of some mix up. They brought her someone else's tray and she had to wait for a new one. In the interim she ate two helpings of stewed prunes, two packages of graham crackers, and a cup of hot tea. When the new tray arrived sometime near two o'clock, it disappeared before I could tell what was on it. There was a blur of activity, and it was gone!!!!

Thanks again for everything and keep praying for us.

Love,

Chuck

10

Push the Easy Button

MY FIRST OFFICIAL DAY OF physical therapy was amazing and a real eye-opener. After briefly talking to me, Stacey put me through a series of tasks using different equipment. I gripped a handrail and walked slowly up three steps, stopping on each, until I reached the top. A red "Easy Button" greeted me. Stacey said, "Push it." After pressing the round button I realized this effort hadn't been too bad, and I repeated the climb two more times. I understood she was preparing me for my discharge, teaching me the little things we all take for granted. I told her steps wouldn't be a problem, since our home was all on one floor.

On the side of the large room was a model of half of a car. Stacey taught me the correct way to get in and out, lowering myself sideways to the seat and then swinging my legs around together until I was facing forward. We practiced several times.

To my amazement, she asked me to get on the treadmill. *She must be kidding!* My apprehension must have shown on my face, since she assured me the speed would be extremely slow with no incline. Cautiously, I stepped on and was pleasantly surprised how well I could accomplish this small task. I guess being an ardent exerciser had made it easier and less intimidating. It felt strange having this sensation of a heavy load pressing on my butt. It was painful, but I resolved to do whatever it took to help myself.

Vanity goes out the window when you're in a hospital. No active wear in this gym. Sporting the latest Johns Hopkins hospital gown with another gown over it as a robe, my two "grenades" pinned to my gown on each side, no makeup, my thick dark brown hair mashed flat, my face still slightly swollen—I found the sight in the mirror a little frightening and a little funny. Why do they think having mirrors is beneficial to a patient's recovery? *Be proud of your accomplishment Susan and forget what you look like. You walked up and down steps today, got in and out of a "car", walked on a treadmill, and worked with a fabulous physical therapist.* I often silently gave myself a pep talk throughout the day, to keep me focused on the "now" and how far I had come, not on looking too far ahead.

Before I left PT, Lisa unlaced my tennis shoes and re-laced them with elastic shoelaces, which would be helpful when I could bend over and tie my own shoes. She encouraged me to wear my tennis shoes if I left my room. "The last thing we want is for you to walk out of your slippers and possibly fall," she told me. I watched her take an electric knife and make small crisscross cuts on the thick foam cushion from my wheelchair, which made an interesting waffle design around the area where I would sit. The modification was to make my cushion more comfortable.

At exactly one o'clock, Lisa came into my room carrying some kind of apparatus to use with my next lesson. Using a reacher, she showed me how to put on hospital pants, which were way too big, without bending down. Sitting on the edge of the bed, I rolled one pant leg of my scrubs up to the drawstring waistband using my hands, grabbed it with the reacher, lowering it down to the point where I could ease my foot inside the pant leg, pulling and unraveling the pant leg with the reacher until I could grab it with my hand to complete the task.

How naïve I was. I packed comfortable summer clothes to wear after my surgery, not realizing how uncomfortable a tight waistband would be with a cumbersome bandage, a swollen back, and skin which was extremely sensitive. My nurse suggested getting some scrubs and I sent my children out on a scavenger hunt to find ones with a drawstring rather than an elastic waistband. In they walked with bags from Wal-Mart, Kmart, and a couple of uniform stores. I had a colorful assortment of scrubs, and enjoyed the exercise of deciding which color fit my mood each day. *Why don't they tell you these little tips ahead of time?*

Lisa watched and reviewed the arm and leg exercises from my handbook, making sure I was doing them properly. She brought me several rubber exercise bands, suggesting I begin with the red, work up to the blue, and then try the yellow. "It's so important to strengthen your upper body, since with this type of surgery your arms and hands will be working overtime to allow you to be more flexible and change position easier. Your nurses have told me they have noticed you practicing on your own which is so wonderful. You can't imagine how many of my patients never follow-up with what they learn in their PT and OT sessions."

When Lisa briefly popped into my room early the next morning, she told me she would help me take a shower and wash my hair after lunch. I could have kissed her. It had been eight days since I showered. Sponge bathing was the only option in these circumstances, but I never really felt clean like I feel after a hot shower. Her news lifted my spirits and gave me something different to look forward to in the afternoon. Eight days is nothing compared to the five weeks I couldn't wash my hair after surgery for a detached retina in 1977 at the Johns Hopkins Wilmer Eye Institute, just nine days after my first son was born. My eyes were bilaterally patched and I wasn't allowed out of bed, so I used to pull my long thick hair back in a ponytail to keep it off my face and keep the "grease" in check.

Keeping up with my rigorous physical and occupational therapy sessions each day was challenging. I knew the more I practiced what I had been taught, the quicker my recovery would be. In between sessions, I would take walks around the rehab floor with Chuck. I knew I needed to get my strength back, but I couldn't believe how tired I was. You would think as active as they were keeping me during the day, I would have slept well at night, but no such luck.

Nights were uncomfortable. Despite all the pillows I arranged around me, I could not find a comfy, restful place for myself. Those damn butt tubes from my drains were more than annoying when trying to sleep on my back, and my right side wasn't much better. Through many trials I figured out the best position for my adjustable mattress, then would put two pillows under my knees, adjust the drains, and will myself to sleep— only to have someone come in and wake me up to take my blood pressure.

I often awoke to the whirling racket of a helicopter landing on the roof above the Children's Center in the middle of the night. The noise never bothered me. I knew it was the sound of "hope." As the engines shut off, I could almost see the trauma team rushing to help a young child, gravely ill or injured in an accident, and I said a silent prayer for healing and recovery.

I have been so amazed and so proud of this premier institution and the medical advances it has given to the world and the patients and families entrusted to its care. I wrote my thoughts in a poem in one of the classes I previously took at the Renaissance Institute at the Notre Dame of Maryland University, which offered non-credit courses for people over fifty.

Rehearsed Anxiety

The call received—
ETA—ten minutes,
a brief history
vital signs
in flight triage,
a deep breath taken—
personnel alerted
preliminary strategies,
a rush to the roof.
The wait endured—
a few more minutes,
standing by
in anticipation
doctors,
nurses
staged in readiness
a gurney,
equipment—
through thick gray clouds
the ominous sound
of an approaching copter—
a silent prayer.
The landing accomplished—
precisely on target
turbulence
the dying whoosh of rotor blades
doors flung opened
controlled mayhem—
a small child in distress
an anguished mother
the transfer—
a dash into the hospital
The vigil of hope begins.

Armed with supplies and a huge smile, Lisa came bouncing into my room, ready to get started with my shower. My desire to feel half-human again overpowered my need to finish the lunch tray sitting in front of me.

"Let me get a few things set up in the bathroom," she said. "I don't want to leave you alone to run back and get something I might have forgotten."

A shower chair with a plastic bed pillow awaited my arrival in this small space. While Lisa held my drains, I carefully took off my hospital gown, slowly maneuvering myself over to the chair, and gently eased myself down onto the pillow. She explained the pillow would keep me from slipping off the wet plastic chair. She then removed the outer wrapping of what appeared to be a large rectangular clear bandage and gently placed it over my existing bulky bandage to keep it dry. A wash cloth, long handled sponge, soap and shampoo were placed within my reach on another chair inside the shower. Lisa gave me explicit instructions on the art of washing my body without standing, bending, or falling.

"Tell me if the water is the right temperature for you," she said, as she removed the hand-held shower head from its overhead position.

At first I just luxuriated in the soothing feeling the warm water gave me as it splashed over my hair and down my body, just allowing my brain to linger in this moment, another tiny step towards normalcy. Lisa washed my hair and stepped outside the bathroom while I did the rest, using the soapy long-handled sponge to reach my back, legs, and feet. I felt a little like a drenched rat as Lisa watched me grab the bar to gingerly pull myself up so I could dry myself. Lisa dried the parts I couldn't reach, smoothed lotion over my body, and told me, "Job well done!" This was such a wonderfully slow process of sequential steps which in our everyday busy lives is another thing we all take for granted.

"Do you want me to dry your hair or are you up for it?" Lisa asked.

"I'll try it," I told her, "but you may have to finish up since I'm really getting tired."

It was a joy to just lean against my walker and see myself in front of the mirror, with normal-sized features, matted wet hair, and a refreshing glow of cleanliness. Before my surgery I had had my hair cut shorter, so it dried quickly even though I was only using my hand to style it. Wearing a clean hospital gown and reverse gown as a robe, I was so happy to see Chuck waiting patiently for my grand exit from the bathroom. He approached me with a big hug. I really wanted to ask him to "smell me", but "I love you" was more in order. Although exhausted, I felt like a new woman.

My bed linen had been changed and looked so inviting. A Snickers bar sat on top of the neatly placed pillows. I didn't have to ask who put it there since Chuck, a master of simple courtesies, was always surprising me with little treats to brighten my day here in rehab just like he did back at home. When I would sit at the computer writing or talking on the phone, a cup of chamomile tea or a square of Trader Joe's rich dark chocolate would mysteriously appear, always bringing a smile to my face and a glow in my heart.

Strictly following the protocol for getting in and out of bed, I had just enough strength to roll myself over onto my back. Chuck had saved my meal tray, but I wasn't interested. He had brought new emails for me to read and a pile of cards that had been delivered to the Pavilion.

"Later darling," I said, half nodding off. "Why don't you go to the gym while I take a nap?"

Leaning over close to me he said, "Get some rest, Sugah. I'm so proud of you."

Another little milestone. I'll just ….

August 7

Hi Folks,

My beautiful wife surprised me today. Adorned in Hopkins' finest, Susan walked out of the bathroom leaning on her walker with a refreshing glow. Her hair was full and shiny, no longer flat from lying in bed for days on end without shampooing it. She had a grin from ear to ear when she saw me, which lit up my heart. This was her first shower since her surgery eight days ago. It's hard to believe we've been here over a week.

Scott and Bridget came to visit after work and brought down a few items I had asked for. Susan was asleep, but when she heard familiar voices outside her door, she called to let me know she was up. She was so glad to see them. She tires easily and has asked only immediate family visit for now. She is trying to rest as much as she can to conserve her energy to keep up with the rigorous schedule they have her on. Susan isn't taking many phone calls either.

Another day, moving forward. Your emails and cards continue to lift her spirits.

Blessings,

Chuck

11

Breakfast Club

Y OU KNOW YOU'VE BEEN IN the hospital too long when you are excited about attending the PT/OT Breakfast Club. I dressed up for the occasion, wearing royal blue drawstring scrub pants and a white blouse with light blue flowers. I even put on lipstick, which was the first thing Stacey and Lisa commented on when I entered the rehab dining room.

There were nine other patients participating in today's event. Their goal was to prepare us for discharge and our return to our homes. They showed us strategies and tips to make everyday tasks less demanding and more efficient. "How are you going to get that box of Cornflakes off the top shelf if you need to use a walker?" Lisa asked. She attached a canvas bag to Yvonne's walker and showed her she could get the cereal off the shelf by using her reacher. Completing that task, Yvonne proceeded to place the cereal in the canvas bag and proudly returned to her table. Mission accomplished.

Each person was assigned a particular task to complete for the whole group. I was in charge of cutting up the fruit. *Sounds like a no-brainer.* Others were setting the table, scrambling eggs, making muffins, pouring juice, and making coffee. I was told the fruit was in the refrigerator, and I was all ready to use my canvas bag. Opening the refrigerator, I was not prepared to see a two-pound bag of apples, several oranges, grapes, and strawberries on the bottom shelf. Thank goodness the bananas were sitting on the kitchen counter. I walked back to my chair, retrieved my reacher, and returned to the refrigerator. I was able to pull the bag of apples up to the next shelf, finally hoisting it up to the top shelf, and carefully dropping it into my canvas bag. The other fruit was so much easier, although reaching for rolling oranges was challenging. Now I understand why they wanted me to practice all the arm exercises to build upper body strength. What a slow process this was, I thought, as I went back to get a large bowl and a knife. Sitting atop the cushion on my wheelchair, I was enjoying the mundane chore of making a fresh fruit salad, often watching the flurry of activity going on around me, delighting in the wonderful smells that were filling the room.

How nice it was to share a meal with other people who were in various stages in their recovery. Some were talkative, others quiet. A few seemed like they did not want to be there and did not engage in conversation. I was so happy this experience wasn't a "let me tell you my entire medical history" pity party. Selfishly, even though I know I am usually an attentive compassionate listener, I just wasn't up for listening to everyone's worst-case scenarios.

I felt a bit lightheaded during breakfast, remembering I had only munched on a protein bar earlier. I'm a breakfast girl, and we were eating much later than normal. It certainly was worth the wait. Hot eggs, toast, hash browns and fresh fruit salad filled my plate. This was so much better than the tray I had been receiving each morning. Sadly, a headache took hold and I had to excuse myself and go lie down. Lisa walked with me back to my room. I was disappointed, but I knew I had learned a lot today.

As usual, Chuck was absorbed in a book when I woke up. His passion for reading and learning is a source of joyful comfort in his life. I didn't want to disturb him. I was enjoying the silence, having him near, and I was grateful for the love we shared. I recalled a poem I had once written for him:

You fill my heart with…

indoor sunsets

lasting rainbows

luminous nights

daises in winter.

Realizing I was awake, Chuck reached for my hand. "Feeling better, Sugah?" he asked.

"Much better," I replied. "Guess I ran out of steam. Everything is such an effort, but I know I'm making progress."

"Stacey came in to check on you earlier," he told me. "She said she would take another patient and come back for your PT after your nap. I saved your lunch."

Uncovering the lid on my plate had become a sort of memory game. Could I remember what I had circled on the menu two days ago? Sometimes I would win, and sometimes revealing what was on the plate surprised me.

"Are you up for a longer walk now?" Stacey asked as she entered my room.

"I feel refreshed. Do you want me to show you the courtyard in The Phipps Clinic Building we talked about?" I asked.

"That's quite a trek and a lot further than I was planning," she said.

"Let's do it while there's not as much pedestrian traffic by the Wolfe Street entrance. You'll love it, and I need some fresh air," I replied.

"Okay, but I'll walk beside you with your wheelchair in case you get too tired. I hope you know we're going for a walk today not a marathon."

"You girls have fun," Chuck said as he kissed me goodbye.

I suggested he take a nap in my bed while I was gone. He looked tired from all this back and forth and sitting and hanging around all day. I was glad he was going to the gym regularly to exercise and maybe relieve some of his inner tension.

To be outside, with the warm summer sun shining brightly overhead through pillows of clouds, a slight breeze against my face, felt fabulous. Walking towards Phipps, I heard someone call "Susan". I turned and there was Eleanor, a friend and receptionist from Neuroradiology. We hugged. "So good to see you," I said. "It's been awhile. How is your family and everyone at Neuro?"

"It's been ages. You look terrific," she said. "Peter told me he bumped into you before your surgery, but I haven't had a chance to get up to visit."

"I haven't been up for many visitors. Just trying to rest and save my energy," I said. "Sorry, forgive my manners. This is Stacey, my physical therapist. We're out for a leisurely stroll."

Realizing we were taking up my allotted PT time, Eleanor and I said our goodbyes. Before she left, Eleanor told Stacey, "Take good care of her. She's one of our frequent flyers here at Hopkins."

Together, Stacey and I glanced up at the inscription on the building: "The Henry Phipps Psychiatric Clinic, 1912." Leaving my walker and holding tightly to the handrail, I cautiously maneuvered each step at the entrance to the building, pausing on each for balance and to gain confidence. It was reassuring to have Stacey by my side.

After leaning me against the brick wall for support, Stacey bounced down the steps to retrieve my walker. One more cement step and we were directly inside the large reception room with its graceful columns, wood paneling, and a beautiful geometric black-and-white-patterned marble floor. An article in the *Hopkins Medical News (2003)* describes the history of this beautiful edifice:

Dedicated in 1913, the five-story Edwardian-style red brick building has been carefully preserved. It was named after Henry Phipps, the Pittsburgh steel magnate who had endowed the clinic. Architect, Grosvenor Atterbury, a champion of aesthetics in hospital design meticulously planned the clinic with sensitivity to beauty. Patients were treated at the world-famous clinic until 1982, when the Meyer Building was completed and Phipps was converted into offices. The building stands as a proud monument to psychiatry's early days as a true medical specialty.

"This is gorgeous—a real treasure," Stacey said. "I've passed this building so many times and never realized what was behind those doors."

"Just wait until you see the courtyard," I said. "It's so beautiful."

Stacey was as amazed as I was the first time I was here. The building is designed to form a U shape, having two wings around a garden courtyard and a cloistered walk with its own fountain, boxwoods and trees. I told her I always thought it would be a great venue for a wedding.

"Since it's used for offices now, what brought you to Phipps?" Stacey asked.

"I used to be a volunteer for the Children's Center Child Life Department and taught their outreach 'Hello Hospital' program in area kindergartens. I visited classrooms and showed a slide presentation about what children might see in a hospital, easing their fears and making them more comfortable and familiar with a hospital environment. It was fun, actually, and was always followed by 'doctor play' with stethoscopes, blood pressure cuffs, needleless syringes, and surgical masks, which the children really enjoyed. Of course today if I walked into a classroom with a slide presentation the techno-savvy five-year-olds would ask me, 'What's that circle thing on top of that machine?'"

We both had a good laugh. I told her we often had our annual brainstorming luncheons in one of the outdoor areas of this building. Chuck and I were here for the ground-breaking ceremony held in this very courtyard for the Charlotte R. Bloomberg Children's Center and the Sheikh Zayed Heart and Vascular Institute Towers.

This outing was wonderful and a real shot in the arm for me, but Stacey could see that I was tiring. "Your choice—the walker or the wheelchair?" she asked.

"The wheelchair until we get to my floor," I said. "Then I'll use the walker to get to my room."

Chuck greeted us in the hallway. "Looks like you had a real girls' day out. Thought I was going to have to call security to find you," he joked.

August 8

Good Morning Everybody,

This update is late because I called it quits early yesterday. I felt really tired. So I turned in around nine o'clock. Susan has a really busy day scheduled again tomorrow.

Sunday was another very good day for her. She continues to work really hard to get back to normal.

Craig and Sonel brought me a care package of food my mother-in-law had made for me. Two huge grocery bags were filled with homemade soups, bagels, lox, cream cheese, and marinated chicken. There also was a banana cake and her delicious mandel nut bread.

The three of us walked over to the hospital just after lunch. Susan was not in her room so I began looking around and guess where I found her? She was up the hall visiting with Patricia, one of the patients that she had met at the "Breakfast Club." There she was, dressed in her black scrubs, and her red

Maryland Terps T-shirt. She loves people and makes friends everywhere she goes. Of course it can be really difficult to get her to talk because she is such a wallflower!

In the afternoon, Susan and her physical therapist went for a really long walk to one of the older buildings in the front entrance of Hopkins. She continues to progress well. Her attitude and her appetite remain very good. Nothing is going to keep her down for long.

Bridget and Scott came to visit in the evening. We were all joking around so much and reminiscing that Susan had to tell them to "cool it" since the laughter was causing more pain.

Thanks again to everyone for your continuing support.

Love,

Chuck

12

Finally!

It was day four of rehab. I believe having a rigorous schedule has helped with my recovery. It's exhausting me, but keeping me focused. What an extraordinary part of the human anatomy your brain is. I marvel at how well your mind can adapt to the routine of a hospital setting and the things people can achieve just through conscious positive thinking.

I was keenly aware of what my limitations were and the challenges they presented. There was a myriad of little things just in my daily personal care which couldn't be done the way I had done them before my surgery. At times it was challenging, coming up with inventive ways to accomplish things I used to take for granted. With my walker by my side, I had no problem washing my face with a washcloth. My arms are long enough to reach the faucet. Since leaning over the sink was not an option, I learned to tuck a towel in front of me like a bib, and splash water on my face, only bending my head. It was a hit or miss process and a bit messy, but it worked. The first time I did this by myself I had to ask my nurse if she could help me change my gown. It was soaking wet. I was learning.

I tried to follow my protocol for exercises on my own at least twice a day when I was in my room, and hoped to build up my strength. Some days my legs felt wobbly, so I was grateful for the walker. The last thing I wanted to do was fall. Just the thought of it sent chills up my spine, since I no longer had a tailbone and only had two of the five parts of my sacrum. I realized the stronger I became, the sooner I could be discharged. Yet, I didn't want the staff to see I was making too much progress, for fear they would discharge me before I was emotionally ready to leave and do all of this on my own. As wonderful as Chuck is, there was security in knowing there was a fabulous medical team there for me if I needed them.

So far no one had given us any indication I would be discharged anytime soon. With only fourteen beds on the unit, I suspected there were many patients who would have loved to have my room. I wanted to go home, but also I wanted to stay where there were so many resources at hand. I hoped there wasn't a Hopkins protocol requiring a patient to have a bowel movement before they could be discharged—if they did, I thought I would be there a very long time. When off my routine, it is not unusual for me to have problems. (In the 70's I went to Europe for eight days, and didn't go to the bathroom until I was back in the United States… and it wasn't for lack of food!)

Chuck and I were scheduled to meet with my rehab team that afternoon. I loved these girls—so helpful, energetic, and compassionate, with a great sense of humor. Rather than a grueling ordeal, it was a joy to work with them. Who would have thought on Day Two, Stacey would challenge me to a game of bowling using the Wii? I thought she had lost her mind, but she told me "lunges" were good for my balance. What fun. I hadn't bowled in decades and was never great at it even as a teenager. I found that my score was much better using a Wii controller than when I had used a ten-pound bowling ball.

With all my efforts, I was still weak and tired very easily. As expected with this type of surgery, the pain can be relentless especially during the night. Night should bring solitude, tranquility, and relaxation. Instead, night was also when the slower pace of the medical setting provided a time for reflection, where symptoms are often magnified, and emotions amplified. Everything seemed to become worse at night. I guess it was the stillness.

That night I wasn't arranging and rearranging pillows to find a comfortable place for my butt; I wasn't dwelling on the pain I was in, or letting my mind wander on the "what if" scenarios about the future. Instead, I was a happy camper since that irritating catheter had finally been removed. No longer would a nurse be rubbing an ultrasound wand over my bladder to measure how much urine was still being retained, something they routinely did several times a day. As my mind wandered in the quiet, dim light, I thought there must be a song for this occasion, but all I could think of was "Happy Days Are Here Again." (As bothersome as the catheter was, I'm sure it must be much worse for a man.) I'm just grateful it's out. Now, I wait.

I called Chuck at 10:45 PM. I knew I would probably wake him, but I just had to share my excitement. "Did I wake you?" I asked.

"No Sugah. I'm just lying here reading," he said. "Are you crying? What's wrong?"

"Nothing's wrong. I'm just a bit weepy. They took the catheter out earlier, and I just tinkled on my own. I wanted to share this good news with you."

"Congratulations Sugah. That's fantastic. Another milestone toward your recovery."

"I can't tell you how grateful I am to feel the urge to void and to know my bladder is in working order, especially after so many of my docs told us what the complications could have been if they had to cut those nerves," I said. "I've had to self-catheterize before and it's not the worst thing in the world, but it's just a nuisance and an inconvenience. I'm ecstatic I won't have to do it again."

"I can hear the excitement in your voice and I'm so happy for you."

"I'm so happy for *us*. Sweet dreams darling. I love you."

13

More Historic News

ALTHOUGH THE NEWS WAS WONDERFUL about probably being discharged soon, I was still a bit apprehensive about leaving. I was looking forward to being a couple again and putting some normalcy back into our lives. The anxiety came from those recurring questions: Am I truly ready? What will happen when we're on our own? How will I deal with the lifestyle changes I need to make? How will this affect Chuck, my primary caregiver?

I focused on what I knew for sure. My surgery was successful. Dr. Wolinsky and his team removed the entire tumor intact without severing the nerves that control bowel and bladder. I reminded myself I was relatively healthy—no heart disease, diabetes, or other major challenges. It's a miracle the stress from the numerous autoimmune conditions I have haven't flared and caused more problems. I focused on the fact that I had an extraordinarily loving and caring husband, who would do anything for me. I brought to mind my fabulous friends and family whose support had been overwhelming. Yet, in spite of all the positives, I was nervous and a bit weepy. *Get control Susan. You're a fighter! You know to look at the glass as half full, not half empty. You can do this. Stay focused. Don't look too far ahead. Take one day at a time. Take only one hour at a time if that's all you can handle. Be your own cheerleader and coach. God has blessed you with the gift of life. What more can you possibly want?*

Good news came while I was trying to detox my head. My nurse breezed in to let me know there is an order to remove one of the drains in my butt. That certainly will help me get back on track. A warm welcome kiss from Chuck also lifted my spirits. Today, his backpack was filled with a bunch of cards, emails he'd printed for me to read at my leisure, and mail our neighbor had sent from Sarasota. So many friends of my children, family, and friends wanted to be added to Chuck's email group to get his updates. The outpouring of love and support warmed my heart and was truly a gift. Healing prayers were being said for me in all types of synagogues and churches, some by people I didn't even know.

He was also carrying a huge box. The return address told me it was from the Miller cousins, first cousins on my father's side, the four I am closest with. Chuck went to the nurses' station to get a scissors after he was unsuccessful opening the box with his keys. After rummaging through the wads of tissue paper, I pulled out this adorable full-sized stuffed bull dog and smiling cat that had their arms around one another. The tag said, "Push here." With a deep boisterous voice the bulldog sang, "If you're ever in a jam, here I am." Then the cat answered in her soprano voice, "If you ever need a pal, I'm your gal." With both heads bobbing together, they harmonized, "It's friendship, friendship, just a perfect blendship. When other friendships have been forgot, ours will still be hot! Lahdle-ahdle-ahdle-dig-dig-dig." What joy these two brought—a little bit too loud for a hospital, but such delightful fun. It was the perfect pick-me-up.

Chuck put my dynamic duo on the window sill after the nurses and other patients had enjoyed my gift. You couldn't help but laugh. I found another surprise buried in the large box and it was marked "For Chuck." Leave it to my cousins to send him a gold star trophy engraved "Star Reporter"...so appropriate. He was truly touched by their thoughtfulness in remembering him. I called Ina at work to thank her for making our day. She said she couldn't make up her mind in the store, since everyone had turned around to see where those loud voices were coming from when she played the jingle.

"I thought it was too noisy for a hospital, but also thought it would be great fun and it would put a smile on your face," she told me.

"It did the trick, alright. I was in a bit of a funk earlier and these characters certainly cheered me up. The whole rehab floor also enjoyed these cuties. I'll call Carole, Arleen, and Renee later."

"I'll tell them you got our gift. You get some rest and take care of yourself. And don't even think about sending all of us thank you notes. Hope you're hearing me."

More history-making good news came later in the afternoon. You wouldn't think two adults could get so excited about a bowel movement—well, not exactly a "movement," but an accomplishment just the same. Although small, painful and extremely hard, it came, as did the tears. Some were from joy; most were from the intense pain. Chuck called Buddy who was driving to Nags Head, North Carolina, with his family, with an update. Then he contacted his daughter, Chris. I called Craig and Scott with the news. All our children probably thought we were nuts, or had just been entrenched in this drama too long to make appropriate decisions. I really didn't care what they thought. I was just happy my bowel still knew what it was supposed to do.

It seemed the urge to have a bowel movement came more often than normal. It still was an effort to get out of bed and sometimes I was exhausted by the time I reached the bathroom. I tried to distract myself by concentrating on a magazine, not on the pain, or what was or was not happening. Despite taking daily stool softeners, Metamucil wafers, and my bran concoction, things were far from normal. *Be patient and grateful, Susan. All your docs told you what to expect. Go with the flow. That sounds ridiculous since there isn't any flow, just a marble here and there.*

They didn't want me to strain, but it felt like the stool was stuck. And the pain was unbelievable. I realized it was magnified because I have lichen sclerosis in that area, a chronic inflammatory skin disorder in which the skin becomes very thin—just another weird autoimmune thing I have. I remembered Dr. Gearhart's words, "Take the enemas!" *Well, they aren't offering me any enemas!*

A few more hours passed. Upon my insistence, Chuck had returned to the Pavilion for some much needed rest. Staying with me wasn't going to make things happen any sooner. Intellectually, I knew I just had to be more patient. Emotionally, I was not handling this well.

By eight o'clock I rang for the nurse, which is something I rarely did. I was in such discomfort. I explained the situation and within the hour Dr. Neufeld, the Rehab resident, was at my side listening intently and said he thought he should take a look.

"Susan, you have a sizable hemorrhoid which is complicating your problem," Dr. Neufeld told me. "I'm going to order a sitz bath for you and a script for Anusol-HC suppositories. I want you to use the sitz baths several times a day. It should help ease your pain." Having my bottom immersed in warm water did sound like a good plan.

"Thanks, Dr. Neufeld. I'm sorry the nurses had to page you over this. At least we know what we're dealing with here and that I'm not crazy."

I was partially awake from a restless night when an unfamiliar aide came into my room at three o'clock in the morning, carrying a sitz bath package. Even though it was the middle of the night I was more than willing to get this show on the road. (It's pretty sad when the patient has to demonstrate how the sitz bath works, because the aide had never used one of these before.)

The warmth of the water felt wonderfully soothing. By intermittently adding more water from the plastic bag which hung above the toilet, the temperature was kept warm and comfortable.

I struggled trying to read a *Reader's Digest* since I didn't have my reading glasses, but I didn't want to bother the aide again. When my sitting limit was up after about fifteen minutes, I called for the aide to help me get back in bed. I drifted off and before I knew it, the neurosurgery residents were asking how I was doing.

August 9

Hi All,

Praise GOD! Another GREAT DAY today! We passed another major hurdle. Susan finally had "somewhat" of a successful bowel movement. She continues being able to void. So her plumbing is working. We are so blessed!

After Susan's morning PT and early afternoon OT sessions, we attended a Rehab Planning Meeting with Stacey and Lisa. They set goals for Susan's continued progress and identified the medical equipment she will need when we leave the hospital.

Her discharge date is set for Thursday, August 13. We are both counting the days until then. I will let you know when she feels she can receive visitors.

We have an appointment scheduled for August 18 with Dr. Wolinsky, the skilled neurosurgeon who performed her operation, after which we can begin planning for our return home to Sarasota.

I surprised Susan with a Good Humor Strawberry Shortcake Popsicle this afternoon. Her eyes lit up when she realized what it was. She was so pleased. She said it was the first one she thinks she has had since she was a little girl. For my reward she gave me a really special kiss. I think I'll take her a whole box tomorrow!

Dave and his youngest son, Drew, came to visit this evening. She was so glad to see them. We took a long walk and showed them the large statue of Jesus, which stands below the dome of the original Hopkins building.

Susan showed me a courtyard on the 3rd floor which is very close to her room. We plan to have a date night there under the stars before she gets discharged.

Once again we send our heartfelt thanks to everyone. Thank you for your support and prayers.

Love,

Chuck

14

"Meanwhile, I Keep Dancing"

A FTER A STRENUOUS DAY, OUR date night began with Chuck asking, "Sugah, will you honor me by joining me for dinner tonight? No wine, no fancy appetizers, no special entrees, just a special night out with my courageous wife and best friend."

"Well, with that wonderful invitation, how could a girl say no?"

Dressed in my purple scrubs and the lime green Hopkins T-shirt we bought on an excursion to the Women's Board gift shop, we took the elevator down to the first floor cafeteria, bought dinner—a foot-long Subway turkey sub stacked with veggies—and went back up to the courtyard. Surprisingly, we had the whole area to ourselves. Chuck and I toasted each other over Diet Pepsi, each with thoughts and words that came from the heart. We talked and reminisced. We laughed and there were a few tears. We licked the gooey chocolate that remained on each other's fingers from the delicious brownie Chuck had bought. We embraced with a passion which had been missing over the past couple of weeks. The sky darkened, but our spirits remained bright. Silently we both were grateful for this moment, realizing how far we had come and how blessed we were.

With little fanfare, I was discharged from rehab two days later. Chuck had taken most of my personal items and things I had accumulated back to our apartment at the Pavilion. After some bittersweet good-byes and a wheelchair escort to the front Wolfe Street lobby, we boarded the Hopkins van for our ride over to the Hackerman-Patz Pavilion. It probably would have been quicker and less bumpy if Chuck had wheeled me over rather than navigating through the snarl of traffic and swarm of pedestrians which were always around the hospital campus.

Sarah greeted me with open arms and a hug. "We're so glad to have you back," she said. "Chuck has been keeping us updated on your progress. Sounds like you were quite a trooper. Let us know if there is anything you need."

It sounds absurd and a little old-fashioned, but I felt like Chuck should carry me over the threshold of our apartment to mark this new beginning in our lives. Since that wasn't an option (and wouldn't be at our age even without the surgery), I pictured my fantasy in my mind as he unlocked the door.

Sunlight streamed through the windows, and provided a warm glow as we entered. It had been over two weeks since I had been there. I was a little surprised to find the apartment spotless and neat; no evidence a man had been living there alone. Chuck confessed he had asked housekeeping if they could clean earlier that day in preparation for my arrival. Chuck put the medications he had picked up at the Outpatient Pharmacy on the small dining table along with my discharge instructions. He put the other medical items Hopkins gave us on the bureau in our bedroom.

"Sugah, you must be exhausted. I can see it in your eyes. Why don't you take a nap while I get a salad ready for dinner? I put clean sheets on the bed this morning and fresh towels in the bathroom."

"You're a gem," I said, throwing him a kiss. "And yes, I am very tired."

I gingerly moseyed into the bedroom with my walker, trying to get a feel for maneuvering on the hardwood floors. I was cautious when using a walker on different surfaces. As they say, rather be safe than sorry. As Chuck turned down the quilt, I spotted an envelope on the pillow. Without opening it, I knew it was from him. A few other envelopes waited for me on the night table.

"The card fairy must have been here," I said.

Chuck smiled as he took off my tennis shoes. Holding his card, I sat on the side of the queen-sized bed. Following the "lift your legs, lean to the side as you lie down" protocol I was taught, I inched myself into a somewhat comfortable position.

I read the message on the card and then the personal one he wrote on the left blank side. I tried to hold back the tears. He had included the words from another card he had given me a long time ago.

I get up.

I walk. I fall down.

Meanwhile, I keep dancing.

—Daniel Hillel

Chuck had used this card as the center of the trompe-l'oeil oil painting he did for one of his art classes. The technique involves realistic imagery in order to create an optical illusion, so the depicted objects exist in three dimensions. It's hanging in our breakfast room, and Chuck tells everyone this painting is about me. It's one of my favorites: a tactile cork bulletin board with two other cards of vivid orange and blue flowers, a stamped envelope addressed to the Johns Hopkins Children's Center, restaurant coupons, Post-it® Notes, and a house key—all attached with painted 3-D push pins. I was a volunteer for the Children's Center, am the Coupon Queen, and tend to leave Post-it® Notes with reminders and romantic messages all over our home. Everyone who visits wants to reach out and touch his painting because it looks so real.

"I need a hug, darling," I said.

Sitting on the edge of the bed, Chuck said, "I don't want to hurt you."

"You won't hurt me. I'm never in any pain when I'm in your arms."

"It's so great to have you back with me. This place has been lonely without you."

The next thing I heard was Chuck calling my name, tapping me on the shoulder to let me know it was time for my medication. I had no idea what time it was, but I could see it was getting dark.

I felt bad I wasn't up for the special dinner Chuck had prepared for me the night before. He understood, and we enjoyed a light meal of soup and salad, and a Metamucil wafer for dessert. As he had been doing every night, Chuck took our dishes to the community kitchen to be placed in the common dishwasher, and brought back clean ones for the next day.

August 13

Dear Friends and Family,

I was discharged from Hopkins today, seventeen days after my surgery. I'm making very good progress but still have a long way to go. It is great to be back at the Pavilion with Chuck. As you well know, he has been my rock and biggest cheerleader during this journey. I feel so blessed to have him and all of you in my life. Your caring and supportive emails and cards have touched my heart and truly helped with my recovery.

Hugs to all,

Susan

That night, sleep eluded me. I don't think it was caused by the nap I had earlier. Despite having the piles of pillows around me and something to help me sleep, I had a hard time finding a comfortable spot. The "wave" machine we had brought with us to try to mask the outside noise on Broadway and Orleans

Streets just wasn't doing the trick, due to the occasional screams of ambulance sirens. When I finally figured out lying on my back with two pillows propped under my legs was the best position, I was able to close my eyes. This was temporary. I slept fitfully. Chuck's slightest movement in our bed intensified my pain and woke me up, as did my two slow trips to the bathroom. I realized we were constantly disturbing each other. Chuck asked if I needed assistance going to the bathroom and I declined each time. I had to try to start doing things by myself. I realized neither one of us was getting much sleep, so I took my book and a bunch of pillows into the living room, closing the bedroom door as quietly as I could.

To no avail, I tried various positions on the light green leather reclining chair in our small living room area. The couch was my only choice. I had sat on this loveseat the first day we were here. Although beautiful, with an attractive and practical print fabric, it was the hardest sofa I ever sat on. When I leaned against the armrest, it gave way and I thought I had dislodged or broken something. To my surprise, I realized the armrest pulled out to expand to a full size couch, and the back cushions could be used to fill in the space which was exposed. The open space revealed a drawer filled with extra sheets, a blanket and pillow. How ingenious, I thought.

I knew I couldn't bend to put on the sheets, so I dropped lots of pillows over the length of the sofa and gingerly lowered myself into a reclining position. Grabbing the blanket off the floor with my right hand, I pulled it over me and said a prayer asking for a couple of hours of uninterrupted sleep.

Chuck insisted on sleeping on that hard couch the next night. No matter how manyw pillows and blankets he laid across the sofa, he was still uncomfortable and wasn't getting a restful night's sleep. We had been so happy to be approved for this suite before my surgery, we hadn't thought about the possible consequences that could occur when I returned after being discharged.

Fatigue continued to plague me. The least little effort wore me out. I thought it was important to get myself into some type of routine with meals, exercise, and short walks planned around my medication schedule. Chuck made a spreadsheet for me to track my meds. (He had been a network planning engineer for Verizon, so we have a spreadsheet for just about anything you can think of.) I must admit his chart certainly came in handy, since lately I had been suffering from "brain fog" and this kept me on track.

Scott came to visit early Saturday evening. Bridget was at a bachelorette dinner. He brought a bag of things we needed that Chuck couldn't get on his weekly van trip to the Safeway in Fells Point. It was great to see him. He apologized for not being able to find a toilet seat riser with support handrails. Earlier in the day he and Bridget had gone from store to store searching for one for our bathroom, so I could safely sit or stand. They had found several different kinds, but none with handrails.

I wished I hadn't told Craig and Sonel it was okay to bring my stepmom down to visit Sunday afternoon. It wasn't anything specific; I just wasn't myself that day. As my dad would have said, "I'm about half." Shirley had wanted to be there during my surgery, but all of us had convinced her not to come since it was going to be a very long day. I knew she was anxious to see me, but as the morning wore on, I started to feel nauseous and a little light-headed.

My cell phone rang as I was about to dial Craig and tell them not to come. They were already in the parking garage. *Well, Susan, you'll just have to make the best of it.* Chuck went down the hall to unlock the garage door on our floor so they could get in. He couldn't wait to get back to tell me that in the corridor he saw the same picture that used to hang above my bed in the condo building where we first met. *And I thought I had the original!*

I loved the muted shades of blues and greens which dominated that watercolor, depicting eleven figures, some coming, some going, all carrying umbrellas as they walked in a light rain through a park-like setting. Street lamps lit their path because of the overcast day. The shapes of their umbrellas lent an oriental feel to the piece. Yet despite the rain, the mood is not somber but more of a peaceful purposefulness, which spoke to me when I bought it. Chuck's news of it being nearby brought it vividly to mind, and, just in the nick of time, its calming effect helped me accept my visitors more gracefully.

Shirley walked in with a cooler filled with food; Craig brought a plant with a beautiful orange blossom, and Sonel was carrying a paisley gift bag with more Trader Joe's dark chocolate. We graciously accepted all contributions to the "Keep the Garbett Refrigerator Well-Stocked" fund. I didn't have the heart to tell Craig the Pavilion didn't allow plants or flowers. Maybe housekeeping wouldn't notice.

"This place is so much nicer than you described in your email," Shirley said. "You are so lucky to be so close to the hospital."

"This apartment has been a God-send for us," I replied, "and has really taken a load off of both of us."

I updated everyone on the latest news from Hopkins and my list of do's and don'ts. "I have a follow-up appointment with Dr. Wolinsky on the eighteenth and will probably receive more instructions at that time," I told them.

As the day wore on, my stomach was becoming more and more queasy. The strong scent from Craig's cologne only made it worse. Time scarcely moved. Lying on the well-padded couch with three people staring at me didn't help matters, although it was great to see family. I wasn't interested in small talk. They realized I wasn't at my best and said their goodbyes. *Thank goodness.*

August 18

Dear Family and Friends,

Sorry there's been a delay in the updates, but I didn't have the best weekend—lots of pain and nausea. Felt better Monday, and we moved our room to one with twin beds so Chuck isn't sleeping on a hard couch. It was a lot of work for him, but worth it to sleep on a real mattress.

Today we saw Dr. Wolinsky, my neurosurgeon. He went over some things with us and answered all our questions. He is still reviewing my tests, and will get back with us shortly. We both really like him and I was grateful he isn't giving us any timetable for returning to Sarasota. He sent us to the plastic surgeon that was part of my surgical team, who removed the sutures and last drain. I can wear a real nightgown tonight instead of a hospital gown!

I appreciate everything everyone is doing to keep my spirits high and help with my recovery.

Hugs to all,

Susan

15

Something's Not Right

THIS IS REALLY QUITE FREAKY, I thought. *Is it a coincidence or a sign?* The light wasn't sufficient for me to read when sitting in the lounge chair, so I pushed the flexible arm lamp that was attached to a small table closer to me. To my surprise, it uncovered a small picture entitled "Lilas de Perse", showing a golden-tan pressed leaf, mounted on hand-made textured paper. It was the exact same piece (one of a pair) which we have hanging in our master bathroom at home. This was the third picture coincidence since we had been at Hopkins. I wondered how many more would be in our future.

I continued to work on building my strength back. It was difficult, especially with nightly interrupted sleep. Many nights I sat on the toilet riser, tears trickling down my cheeks. I brushed them away. Despite the continuing sitz baths and the Anusol suppositories, the pain from the hemorrhoid, lichen sclerosis, and extremely hard stools was intense. Even warm water enemas weren't helping much.

Chuck was doing everything. He was the ultimate caregiver; cooking, doing laundry, shopping, and helping me with my daily needs. I didn't want to wake him up at night so I tried to quietly fill the bag for the sitz bath by myself, but failed to clamp it properly and we had water all over the floor. In a stupor and without complaining, Chuck methodically soaked up the mess with some towels. I felt so bad, but I couldn't bend or be of any help.

At the first sight of dawn I awoke, my mind drifting in a hundred directions. Today would be much like the others: breakfast, meds, exercises, shower, writing a few thank you notes, rest, lunch, more meds, exercise, a short walk, a nap, reading, dinner, more meds, and a little TV. It had become a pattern and I was grateful for the small steps I was taking towards my goal of going home.

Baltimore can be quite hot and humid in August, so Chuck and I were pleasantly surprised how comfortable it was during our slow walks up and down Orleans to Wolfe Street and back again. At times there was even a breeze, so unusual for this time of year.

How we enjoyed our strolls together, watching the ongoing construction and bustle at the new Charlotte R. Bloomberg Children's Center. The vibrant colors and patterned glass that enveloped the façade were designed by contemporary artist, Spencer Finch, who was inspired by the impressionist artist, Claude Monet, and his painting, *The Japanese Footbridge,* painted in 1899. Finch's shades of green, blue, purple, yellow, and gray enhanced the architectural curvature of the building and were just breathtaking. It was such a delight to see this project come to fruition, a dream of so many in the pediatric field.

Sarah, who was sitting at the front desk, handed us a bag from Edible Arrangements that had been delivered while we were out. A beautifully wrapped plaid box with decorative red bow was inside. Since everyone wanted to see what I received, I opened it before going back to our room. Wow! I uncovered a huge box of dark-chocolate-covered strawberries and apples from my stepdaughter, Chris, and her family in Richmond. Nothing like rich, decadent chocolate to make your day! Everyone was delighted when I shared some with the staff.

I felt strangely melancholy when I woke up on that cloudy Thursday morning. I couldn't account for or pinpoint the restlessness I was feeling. Chuck had left a note on top of the package of maple sugar oatmeal on the counter, letting me know he went to the gym and would be back shortly. Next to it was a cup with a green-tea bag waiting to be brewed. I couldn't believe I had not heard him leave. It had been another rough night. I think the pain from attempting to have a bowel movement was worse than the pain from my surgery, if that was possible.

Before Chuck returned, I called Dr. Gearhart's office, hoping she could recommend something to give me some relief. As luck would have it, she was on vacation. I explained my situation to whomever answered the phone and she politely assured me my message would be given to the person covering for Dr. Gearhart, and that someone would get back with me that morning.

Having little appetite, I ate a bagel for lunch. It was well after two when the phone call came from Dr. Gearhart's office. They would have a prescription waiting for someone to pick up at the desk on the sixth floor of the Blalock building. Chuck was listening to my conversation, and was almost half way out the door before I hung up. He was familiar with Blalock, since it was near the Child Life Department which he had been to many times.

The phone rang as I gazed out my bedroom window. I thought it must be cooler outside since I saw people in long-sleeved shirts and light jackets scurrying up and down Broadway to their destinations in the hospital. The caller ID showed it was my friend, Pam, from Sarasota.

"So how are ya?" Pam said in her best Boston accent.

"I'm doing pretty well, but today is not my best day."

"What's going on?" she asked.

"I'm just not myself today. I just don't feel right, and I can't seem to pull myself out of this funk I'm in."

"Listen to me, Susan. You've just been through the fight of your life up there. It's only been a couple of weeks since your surgery. You were told yours would be a long recovery. Give yourself and your body a break. You know you don't have to put on a charade for me."

With those words, the flood gates opened and Pam let me cry over the phone without interrupting. I guess over the past month since my diagnosis, I had been so consumed with finding a surgeon, planning, organizing, closing our home, getting to Hopkins, keeping up pretenses for Chuck, family and friends, and going through the trauma of my surgery, I had not given myself the opportunity to let my guard down and grieve. I was grateful for Pam's wisdom and friendship, and glad Chuck wasn't there to witness how emotionally spent I really was. At the end of our conversation, Pam told me she would keep in touch and to call her any time I needed to vent.

For some reason, Chuck wasn't able to fill my prescription at the Outpatient Pharmacy in the hospital and had to trek over to the pharmacy on the corner of Wolfe and Monument Streets. He called and told me not to expect him anytime soon, since there was a huge line of people ahead of him.

As the day wore on I was feeling worse. I had a dull headache, but I knew that wasn't the primary cause of my problem. Without warning, I started to get chills. I put on my heavy robe and lay down, covering myself with a couple of blankets. My body began to shake excessively, but calmed down within a few minutes. Then I became extremely hot, I thought due to the amount of blankets I had on. Throwing off the blankets and removing my robe didn't help. This was definitely worse than any hot flashes I had experienced. My body appeared to be in some sort of tumultuous upheaval, settling down slowly and then intensifying again. The next hours were overwhelmingly uncomfortable, as my body temperature alternated between intense cold and heat.

The phone rang in the middle of all this. I just assumed it was Chuck and I answered, "Hello Darling."

"It's not your darling, it's Helaine."

"I'll have to call you back some other time. I really don't feel well."

I decided to stick it out and not call Chuck and alarm him. I figured it shouldn't be too much longer before he came home. I was glad I didn't eat much for lunch, because I was getting nauseous. The room reeled and tilted from this volatile turmoil that had taken over my body. It would slowly settle and rebound again, but the intensity was definitely getting worse.

I had no idea what was going on, but I definitely knew something wasn't right. Chuck finally came in around 4:15. He had been at the pharmacy for almost three and half hours. He looked tired, but took one look at me and asked what was going on.

I gave him a brief explanation as he felt my head. Surprisingly, the thermometer indicated my temperature was normal. *How bad could this be if my temperature was okay?*

"Do you think I should still go to Safeway?" he asked. "We have quite a lengthy list."

"Stay with me, baby," I whimpered. "I feel awful."

"Sugah, it's going to be okay," he assured me as he sat down on the couch next to me. He held me close and as much as I tried to hide the shakes, I could tell Chuck was acutely aware of what was going on. "I'm not going anywhere. I'm calling Dr. Wolinsky's office."

I looked at my watch. "It's after five. No one will be in his office."

"I'm calling anyway. Someone must be on call or covering after hours."

Chuck dialed Dr. Wolinsky's office and got a number for the neurosurgery resident on call. He left an urgent message, hoping his call would be returned quickly. We waited. The bouts between cold and hot continued, some for a longer duration.

"Do you want anything to eat or drink?" Chuck asked.

"Don't mention food to me. Just fix something for yourself. You've had a long day."

During all this we totally forgot about the prescription Chuck had waited so long for. I opened the bag and looked at the box. Chuck saw my disappointment.

It was the same Anusol suppositories I was already using. I knew when I talked to the person in Dr. Gearhart's office that I was specific about what med I was already using. Right then I couldn't even think about it.

Three hours passed. "Chuck, please take me to the emergency room. My insides are shaking."

"I know we're only a couple blocks from the ER, but I'm calling an ambulance. You're in no shape to go in a wheelchair."

He notified the front desk to expect an ambulance shortly and asked them to direct the paramedics to our room. I grabbed his hand while he was on the phone.

Although I have toured Johns Hopkins emergency room before, nothing prepared me for the organized chaos that occurs in this big city hospital. For many, it's the neighborhood doctor's office; for others it's the life-saving center for traumas, accidents, and illnesses.

One paramedic rolled my gurney to the side of the hallway to avoid the back-up of other patients, or from bumping into staff running to and from patient's rooms. The other paramedic made his way to the center of the huge room to the nurses' station where information was being inputted into computers, conversations were taking place between staff, and the sounds of phones ringing could be heard.

I closed my eyes, trying desperately to will away this havoc that was happening and gain some control back. It was an effort in futility. Having Chuck gently rubbing my arm was comforting. Eventually I was placed in a small room, my vitals taken again, and an IV started.

The nurse asked us questions as to when symptoms started, had any symptoms changed during the episodes, how long had they lasted, and so forth. She was a "stitch" and before long had us laughing. I guess you have to have a pretty good sense of humor to work in the ER. Between the shakes and the laughter I had the urge to use the bathroom.

"Do you think you can walk there?" she asked.

"Probably with help and my walker," I replied.

I had only taken a few steps before I said, "I'm not going to make it."

She immediately grabbed a bedpan, bent over, held it under my gown as I held on desperately to my walker. With gravity pulling, there was no stopping the flow. It kept coming; I don't know from where, as my nurse steadied the bedpan against my walker for what seemed like forever.

"You weren't kidding you had to go."

"I'm just grateful I feel the urge to go and Dr. Wolinsky didn't have to sever the nerves that control bladder and bowel." I don't know how she was able to hold the bedpan that long. It was embarrassing.

"Would you please do me a favor and check my husband's blood pressure? He has a heart condition, has had a long, trying day, and is now worrying about me. I'm concerned."

Sure enough, his pressure was elevated and the nurse found him a chair.

My shaking episodes were less frequent and of shorter duration. We were waiting for someone from neurology to come to make a determination whether to admit me. We waited and waited. *What a nightmare!*

August 21

Hey Everybody,

Thursday was not the best for Susan or me. As you know, she has been in considerable pain since her surgery on July 28. Yesterday she began having bouts where one minute she was hot, then the next she was very cold and shaking. I checked her temperature twice and it was OK. She didn't feel much like eating and also experienced nausea practically all day.

Last night around 8 PM we called for an ambulance and went to the emergency room. Conditions there were very uncomfortable to say the least. After initially being placed in an examining room where she was given an IV, something for nausea and something for pain, she was moved out of the room and placed in the aisle right in front of where the resident on duty was stationed and where some nurses input data to their computer systems. I had a chair next to her. Whatever was going on inside caused her to urinate frequently. Staff was attending to more severely ill patients, so I walked to the bathroom with Susan several times during the night. It was an ordeal for both of us. Although we were both exhausted, it was impossible to get any sleep with so much going on around us.

We were waiting for someone from the neurology department to come to make a determination whether Susan should be admitted. We waited about 3 1/2 hours before the neurosurgeon on call showed up (this was around 2 AM). She ordered a CT scan and we didn't see her again until around 4 AM. She reported that it looked like Susan was suffering from an abscess, a pocket of infection deep inside where she had had her surgery. One ER doc told us they may have to go back in. That was pretty unsettling.

110

We were moved out of the aisle and returned to one of the emergency room examination areas shared by three other patients. We were so happy to see Dr. Clarke walk in, someone we knew, who had assisted in Susan's surgery and was more familiar with her case. She examined Susan and ordered an MRI to confirm the diagnosis. She didn't believe that there was an abscess, only a pocket of air. Susan was a real trooper. She willed herself to remain still during these long scans, which I'm sure was quite difficult since the bouts of cold and hot had not completely ceased.

At one point, they were sending Susan to another part of the hospital when it was determined by the transport person that she was being sent to the wrong room. Later, Susan was moved to an Emergency Room critical care unit on the 6th floor where she shared a room with a gentleman until a regular room in the neurosurgery department would be made ready.

All in all, it took approximately 14 hours before Susan finally was assigned and situated in a room on the 8th floor in the neurology/neurosurgery section. This is a very nice private room on the same floor where she was originally sent after her surgery. We already know a lot of the nurses and I know my way around. A plastic surgeon examined her and says he doesn't believe that the pocket is as deep as earlier suspected. He indicated that a new drain would be placed.

After she was settled in, I went home and crashed for about 2 1/2 hours and then went back to the hospital around 6:30 PM. Susan had barely touched her dinner. The doctors had started her on one type of antibiotic earlier and then decided to switch to something else. She still is experiencing some pain and bouts of hot and cold and nausea. I left her for the evening around 7:45 PM. We are both exhausted.

The plan is to follow through with a complete antibiotic regimen and to insert a new drain to the pocket. Once the drain is in place and things settle down a little, Susan will be released. This could happen as early as tomorrow.

Please keep us in your thoughts and prayers.

Thanks for the support.

Love,

Susan & Chuck

16

No More Food Commercials

I WAS EXAMINED AND INTERVIEWED BY Dr. David Thomas, Chief of Infectious Disease, along with his resident, Dr. Christensen, for antibiotic management. "The MRI and CT reported a fluid collection at the surgical site," he said. "Additionally, there was a suggestion on the MRI of osteomyelitis [a bone infection caused by bacteria or other germs] in the remaining sacrum, more pronounced at S2." Dr. Thomas started me on a regimen of IV Vancomycin, Cefapime and Metronidazole. I think they were bringing out the "Big Guns" until they figured out exactly what was going on.

I was miserable and extremely nauseous. I couldn't even think of food, which worried Chuck. I was just lying in bed trying not to moan and upset him. I turned off the television I used as a diversion. I found the food commercials irritating. Just thinking about food and seeing all those happy people munching and crunching away at their favorite delights made me turn green.

August 24

Hi Everyone,

I guess I was a little bit over-optimistic when I sent out my last update. From what I was being told, I really expected to have Susan home with me by Sunday at the latest. I was wrong. Things move particularly slowly in a hospital when you have to stay over a weekend.

Anyway, Susan continues to experience bouts of nausea. We believe that most of this now is being caused by the medicines she is receiving by IV. She had not been allowed any regular food until this evening's dinner because some type of procedure was being planned. Apparently there was a disagreement on which type of procedure to use, so the decision changed several times before something was finally agreed on.

The powers to be decided it was not necessary for drains to be placed. Instead, their plan for tomorrow was to draw off some fluid using a needle guided by ultrasound. A biopsy would also be taken from the surface wound. Both of these samples would be tested for infection and would be used to determine the most effective antibiotic to kill whatever is present.

We asked Susan's neurosurgeon if there were any results from the blood cultures taken the other day and he reported that no infection has appeared as of this morning. Susan has not displayed any signs of fever, her temperatures have all been normal. Her white blood cell count is not elevated. She continues to experience pain from her surgery, but she and I walked three circuits around the floor today, this morning and this evening. She feels a lot better today than yesterday, but I know that the nausea and just lying around is getting very old. The feeling of not knowing what to do to help her is very frustrating for me.

She and I watched the first quarter of the Ravens-Jets game together before she shooed me out for the evening. Go Ravens!!!!!!!!! Both of us wish we could have been at Gecko's tonight to be with our friends in Florida. I'm going back to watch the rest of the game as soon as I finish writing this update, which I believe is right now!

Susan and I send everyone a big hug and thanks for the continuing outpour of support. It really means a lot to us. Please continue to remember us in your prayers.

Love,

Susan & Chuck

Results were pending on the guided-needle fluid aspiration done a couple of days prior, along with a wound swab taken at the surgical site. It had been a relatively easy procedure that was done in a dimly lit room, while several onlookers observed and asked me questions.

In between my waves of misery, I paid attention to my reactions to the clear bags of IV fluids the nurses periodically changed during the day. I became convinced it was the Cefapime that was aggravating my nausea, and although I was weak, I boisterously voiced my observations to anyone who would listen. I imagined this nausea (although probably not the best comparison) was similar to chemotherapy side effects for other cancer patients. I now have a heightened understanding and compassion for what they go through as they undergo treatment. Dr. O'Connor was right when she told me, "The good thing about chordomas is you won't need chemo."

I couldn't have been more delighted when Dr. Thomas, after hearing my plea, agreed to discontinue the Cefapime and Metronidazole. I've been hospitalized a lot over the years, and the one thing I've learned is you have to speak up and be your own advocate, or have someone to be your voice.

He planned to start IV CiproFloxin and Vacomycin for a course of six weeks. Panicking, I asked, "Does that mean I'll be hospitalized for another six weeks?" Dr. Thomas assured me this could easily be accomplished as an out-patient by implanting a PICC line (a peripherally-inserted central catheter in the upper arm), which usually works very well for prolonged antibiotic IV treatment.

He told us they would help arrange for this to be done in Sarasota if desired. Dr. Thomas gave us the name of an infectious disease doctor in Florida whose practice is not far from our home. *What a relief.* The thought of being hospitalized any longer than necessary, or having to stay in Baltimore for out-patient IV therapy wasn't on my radar or very appealing. Although I enjoyed seeing my family, I was anxious to go home.

August 25

Hey Everyone,

Yesterday, after a very frustrating early morning and afternoon, things began to turn around. We saw a doctor from the Infectious Disease group and convinced him that a large part of Susan's nausea was caused by the two antibiotics she had been taking. He said that he would order them stopped and placed Susan on a new antibiotic that would not cause her nausea (Ciprofloxacin). A nurse came in about an hour after he left with a new dose of the old medicine.......which we refused. From that time on until I left last night around 8 PM, you could see Susan improving. They did not start the new antibiotic until sometime during the night. At our morning wakeup call I could tell that Susan had really begun to turn the corner.

Susan was able to cautiously resume a regular diet today and we made several walks around the floor. She also walked with a nurse a couple of times while I went to the gym and home for lunch.

Today was a very good and very busy day for Susan. On four separate occasions, doctors from neurosurgery (her team leaders) came in to check on her progress. Later in the day, two oncologists came to review her case.

The lead doctor from Infectious Disease examined Susan. He is the one who issued the orders changing her medications. He also made arrangement to have a "PICC" placed (this is a semi-permanent IV arrangement through which the new antibiotic will be infused). Susan can wear this when we return to Florida before the total antibiotic regimen is completed.

A Discharge Coordinator came by and went over some issues with us. She is going to gather a copy of all the reports from all procedures, test results, etc. for us to carry with us when we return home.

This infection has delayed our initial plans for our return to Sarasota. Now, it looks as if we will return sometime during the week after Labor Day.

Thanks again for your prayers and support.

Love,

Susan & Chuck

17

Music to My Ears

T HE NEXT DAY WAS A new and fascinating experience. After lunch, I was greeted by a male and female nurse, both completely garbed in blue from head to toe. They were my cheerful PICC team, and explained everything about the procedure and what exactly they were going to do. After having me sign a release form, they told me they would insert a long, slender, flexible tube into a peripheral vein in my upper arm. Using ultrasound they would advance it until the catheter tip ends up in a large vein in the chest near my heart to obtain intravenous access. They told me PICC insertions are less invasive, have fewer complications associated with them, and can remain for a much longer duration than other central or periphery access devices.

After taking measurements of my arm and the distance to my heart, they proceeded to drape me and my entire bed with more blue coverings, explaining this was to keep things as sterile as possible. As I watched them put layer upon layer over me, I kept thinking what all this stuff was going to do to the environment—I was pretty sure it wasn't biodegradable. The procedure was a bit uncomfortable, but it didn't take that long for them to achieve the results they wanted. Afterward, I had two leads coming out of my left arm.

Chuck was surprised that my PICC line was already inserted when he came into my room. I was feeling so much better since being taken off the Cefapime. My appetite had returned, my outlook had improved, and I felt the worse was behind me. Except for the soreness in my hand and arm from changing my IV a couple of times, I was doing quite well, although still weak.

That afternoon a woman from nursing services came in to explain what would happen when I was discharged. *Discharged. Yes!! Music to my ears.* Chuck's smile told me he was just as elated as I was.

She demonstrated how to clean the PICC site, screw on the medication container that resembles a light bulb, and gave us other tips for Chuck to learn to do twice a day once I left Hopkins. "If you can screw in a light bulb, you can handle this," she said. I asked her if that was one of those Polish jokes—and then sheepishly asked her if she was Polish as to not offend her. Arrangements would be made for a home-health nurse to come to the Pavilion several times during the week to check vitals and to make sure Chuck was following the procedure correctly. The Vancomycin would be also delivered to the Pavilion. She left her business card and told us to contact her if we had any questions.

August 28

Dear Family and Friends,

I wouldn't recommend getting better too quickly in the hospital. It seems that only a couple days ago I was the sickest I have ever been from the antibiotics they were giving me. When two were stopped, I rallied and some of the nausea stopped and I was able to eat, but was very weak. A PICC was placed yesterday for out-patient IV therapy. Last night Hopkins discharged me at 8:30 PM with a load of papers, quick explanations, and a wave good-bye. It's really weird leaving the hospital at night, but it was great to be back with Chuck in our apartment.

I have a few restrictions. No mountain climbing, horseback riding, roller blading, etc! For real, the list includes no lifting more than 10 lbs., no driving, or alcohol, avoid straining and strenuous activity, and do not take a bath or swim until cleared by my neurosurgeon. I can shower and wash my hair, but should not rub, scrub or soak the wound site for 3 weeks.

Today the home-care nurse came to show Chuck how to administer my antibiotic regimen. It's an easy procedure and Chuck is well prepared and has no problems administering my meds. The meds were delivered last night. They weren't kidding when they told us, if you can screw in a light bulb, you can do this type of therapy. Twice a day I have IV treatments and one oral med. It easy and you can walk around with the tubing bulb in your pocket.

Arrangements were made at Hopkins for home-health care in Baltimore and then again in Sarasota when we return. There's an infectious disease center about twenty-five minutes from where we live. We're looking to return to Sarasota sometime after Labor Day, when I get my strength back and hopefully can sit better.

Thanks again for your prayers and good wishes. They were a blessing when my spirits were low.

Love to all,

Susan

18

Last Week in Baltimore

MY LAST WEEK IN BALTIMORE was tiring but fantastic. Our cousin Renee picked us up in front of the Pavilion and drove us to Fells Point where her husband, my aunt and uncle, and two other cousins were waiting for us for dinner at the DuClaw Brewing Company on the Bond Street Wharf. It was slow-going, but I was determined. It felt great to be out. In a charming old-warehouse atmosphere, we had a chance to catch up a bit, share fond memories, laugh a lot, and enjoy a great meal. Feeling a combination of exhilaration and exhaustion, I headed straight to bed when we returned to the Pavilion. I awoke to the sound of someone softly calling my name. It was time for my IV therapy.

My dear friends, Arlene and Helaine, brought lunch down a few days later; several varieties of delicious wraps, more than enough for us to have another meal back in our apartment. These women are what I call "my middle of the night friends"—those you can count on if you showed up at their home in the middle of the night, those who would not ask questions or be judgmental, those who would just be there, offering you a couch, a blanket, or a teddy bear if you needed one. My younger son, Scott, once told me, "I thought I needed to have a ton of friends when I was in high school, but now that I'm older, I realize if you have a few really good dependable friends, Mom, that's all you really need." He was so right.

Chuck was doing everything in preparation for our departure, organizing and sorting things we had accumulated over the past six weeks, figuring out how we were going to travel with the extra medical equipment, preparing meals that would use up food in the refrigerator and freezer, catching up on any last minute laundry, obtaining permission from Air Tran and BWI airport security to take liquid IV therapy supplies onboard, and making arrangements for our arrival in Sarasota. My job, since I couldn't bend, was to secure plane tickets, make arrangements for a wheelchair at both airports, pay any outstanding bills, and oversee Chuck's efforts and answer any questions that he may have. It's quite obvious who had the heavier burden.

I had a great need to make time to say goodbye to Dr. Wolinsky and his Nurse Practitioner, Laura Blanchfield, before we left Baltimore. Laura was the liaison between Dr. Wolinsky and his surgical patients, helping with medical management of patients before and after surgery. She is a gem and we welcomed her expertise when we had questions or concerns throughout my recovery. It was a great relief having a go-to person when Dr. Wolinsky wasn't available because of his surgery or clinic schedule.

Two days before our departure, we walked up to the outpatient clinic, not knowing if we could see them since we didn't have an appointment. Luckily they graciously took a few minutes to talk to us between patients. As Dr. Wolinsky was chatting, I found myself staring at his hands. They looked like average men's hands… nothing really special about them, nothing that indicated their extraordinary skill, and the healing, and hope they brought to so many. They both wished us well and said I had made wonderful progress. A mere *Thank you* seems inadequate for someone who recently saved your life, but their smiles reflected the gratitude I was trying to convey.

The walk back to the Pavilion was harder, not so much because I was tiring, but more because I was leaving with mixed emotions. I was elated to be going home, yet I was apprehensive about leaving the security Johns Hopkins had provided. And I was concerned about the plane ride home. *How will I handle going through security, sitting for over two hours during the flight, maneuvering in the plane and the bathroom, with all this pain?* I took a deep breath and tried to put these thoughts at bay as we continued our slow stroll down Broadway towards the Pavilion.

Back in our apartment, I told Chuck I thought I was too exhausted to go out to lunch with my aunt, uncle and stepmom.

"Sugah, I thought the trek to see Dr. Wolinsky might be too much for you, but I know how important it was to you to see him before we left. We should have taken a wheelchair instead of the walker. I think you should call Aunt Roz and cancel."

"I'll be okay if I take a nap before they come, but I'm going to ask her to pick up something instead of going out."

I woke to the sound of voices coming from the other room. What a sight! There they stood (all in their eighties), with Aunt Roz holding a picnic basket, Uncle Gordy carrying a cooler, and Shirley clutching a Trader Joe's shopping bag with that famous red and blue UTZ potato chip bag peeking out. I knew my Aunt Roz was behind this effort—the ultimate Jewish mom where no one ever left her home without a bag of goodies. How delightful it was to see them, knowing tackling the drive to the Hopkins campus and finding a parking space can be a bit frustrating. Aunt Roz didn't let my walker keep her from giving me the biggest hug. Teary-eyed, she said, "Suz, you look wonderful. So glad we got to see you before you go home."

"I'm so happy to see all of you. Sorry I had to cancel our lunch outing, but it looks like you outdid yourself as always."

After giving them the tour of our small apartment, we headed to the community dining area. Aunt Roz proceeded to pull out sandwiches she had made from whatever she had in her refrigerator; turkey, cheese, roast beef, and tuna on rye or wheat bread, with chips, pickles, cut-up fruit and vegetables, cookies, and some mandel bread she had in her freezer.

"Aunt Roz, I can't imagine what kind of spread you would have brought if you had more notice," Chuck said. "We really appreciate this."

So we ate, chatted, shared old memories, and enjoyed that special moment. Knowing their ages and how fragile life is, made this time even more meaningful. The Miller family on my father's side has always shared a unique bond which has kept us close even though many live long distances apart. That stability has been a constant in my life, one I truly cherish.

Scott surprised me by popping in to say goodbye after his meeting in downtown Baltimore. Of course, Aunt Roz wanted to know if he wanted a sandwich, and even though he said he just came from a lunch meeting, she showed him the choices she'd brought. Since Scott hadn't seen them in a while, he filled everyone in on what was going on in his life, answering questions and enjoying our time all together.

I clung to Scott before he left to get back to work in Rockville, not wanting to let go, savoring the moment. It wasn't like I wouldn't see him or be able to hug him again; I just had this great need to hold on to him as long as I could. Was this just motherly instinct, or my overwhelming emotional realization that I was still going to be a part of my sons' lives? I felt so grateful. Only a few months before there had been a real possibility this could have ended very differently.

August 31

Dear Friends and Family,

Chuck and I made arrangements to return to Sarasota on Sept. 6. It's been a long journey beginning in Jacksonville on June 25. It will be great to be back in our own home, in our Sleep Comfort bed, and to begin to put some normalcy back into our lives.

Chuck continues to be the wonderful husband and man that he is; administering my IV meds like a pro, doing laundry, grocery shopping, fixing meals, and picking up all the things I drop on the floor.

The final pathology report was presented at the Tumor Board. It showed a chordoma with positive margins of dedifferential, meaning that the tumor showed some very early sarcoma components, which is a more aggressive tumor. Because of this, my doctors feel the need to treat this more aggressively and be pro-active with my care. I will have an MRI twice a year, and will probably be going to Mass General in Boston for proton beam radiation after I heal more. What's in my favor is the tumor was removed intact and is no longer there. My doctors want to keep it that way.

I talked to Dr. Wolinsky about the bowel issues I am having. He told us that the rectum is normally attached to the sacrum. Since most of my sacrum was removed, this may be causing my difficulty with bowel movements. I am just happy it works!

So my book, <u>Susie and Me Days: Joy in the Shadow of Dementia,</u> won't be ready for this year's Alzheimer's Memory Walk on Oct. 24, but I look forward to getting it published in between all this medical stuff.

With love and gratitude for the special people in my life,

Susan

Just before leaving Baltimore, I received an email from my brother. On the subject line it read: "Who and What You Are." Like many siblings, we have had our ups and downs over the years, not seeing eye-to-eye, not exactly being on the same page, but always compromising and forgiving.

Susie,

Of course you had to have the operation, that's a no brainer. But how you carry yourself and your demeanor makes you the incredible woman that you are. There is no braver person that I know and everyone who knows you sent their energy and their love and hope for your complete recovery. You always hold your head high and bring your energy to everyone around you.

Many people look up to you because of the woman you are and the dignity and respect that you have earned throughout your life. You are kind, caring, and give your love freely and openly to everyone near you, especially the needy. If that was not enough, the energy and love that you and Chuck create together is truly known to everyone you know and many you don't know. Dad was always proud of you, and I am too. I tell everyone how much I adore my sister and how much you mean to me. You are a very special woman.

Dave

Except for an unpleasant encounter with a pompous and insensitive Air Tran ticket agent at Baltimore-Washington International Airport, our flight home was surprisingly uneventful. "One of your bags is one pound overweight," she told me. "That will be an extra thirty-nine-dollar charge. Do you want to put it on your credit card?" *What! We're already paying twenty dollars for each piece of luggage and you want to charge us another thirty-nine dollars because we are only one pound over?*

Chuck was no longer with me. He had just placed the luggage on the shelf in front of the check-in counter when he received a call from his cardiologist in Sarasota, and ran to find a quiet spot away from all the hub-bub. I had to handle this myself. Using a calm, controlled voice, although I didn't feel in control at all, I attempted to explain my situation to this young woman. I was told I could remove or shift an item to another suitcase to comply with their weight requirements. I understood her position, but she wouldn't even listen to mine. I wanted to scream! I attempted to make my case. "Check my suitcase," I said, looking up at her from my wheelchair. "It's filled with medical supplies. I can't bend over due to a rare, complicated surgery." My efforts fell on deaf ears. Exasperated, I finally gave up. *What's another thirty-nine bucks when our bills will probably be astronomical?*

"Did everything go smoothly?" Chuck asked when he returned.

"We'll talk on the plane. I'm anxious to get through security," I replied.

The line-up of ready wheelchairs at the gate when we arrived in Sarasota was notable. I had to wait my turn. I remember waiting at the gate to board a flight on one of our trips to visit family in Baltimore and Richmond. Two young boys carrying backpacks were deplaning with their parents. One said to the other, "There's nothing but old people in this airport!"

Once seated in the wheelchair, we took off, not waiting for an escort. Chuck piled a few items and the cooler with my IV supplies on my lap, and quickly pushed me through the airport.

How wonderful it was to see our friends, Jeanne and Alan, waving to us from beside the Mote Aquarium display tank in the waiting area. It was joyous, emotional and overwhelming. Just hearing the words, "Welcome home," opened the flood gates and the tears began to flow. I collected myself as we headed outside. Sarasota never looked so beautiful, with clear blue sunny skies, colorful flowers and tall palms waving in the warm breeze along University Parkway. I took a deep breath, savoring the moment, delighting in the splendor surrounding me.

Finally, after the longest journey of my life, we were home. Even though physical therapy had taught me the proper way to get in and out of a car, it was still no easy feat. Chuck had the walker ready, and I gingerly slid out of their SUV with Chuck and Alan's assistance.

More tears…our neighbors had put a "Welcome Home" sign on our front door. I was so tired, yet exhilarated. Cay, our neighbor across the street, had opened our front hurricane shutters. She later told us, "After all you've been through, I couldn't have you come home to a dark house." There was a pot of soup and a Pyrex dish of baked ziti sitting on the stove, a gift from Maria, our Italian neighbor and self-appointed community guardian. Later, Jeanne told me Cindy, another close friend, had gotten the key from Cay and filled our refrigerator with dairy, produce, deli, and a few dishes she had made.

"We're home, Sugah," Chuck said, cautiously wrapping his arms around me. Leaning against him for support, I felt the wetness from his tears as he tenderly kissed me.

It felt somehow quite strange as I walked from the kitchen through our darkened great room and sat on the waiting couch. Everything looked the same—I don't know what I was expecting. Why would anything look different? It wouldn't be like Cay, who was checking on our home these past months, to rearrange our house. I struggled to make sense of why things seemed odd, though nothing was actually changed at all. I felt like I was having an out-of-body experience. I think the reality that I had made it through and I was finally home had overwhelmed me. I just wanted to sit there and take it all in.

The loud sound from Chuck opening hurricane shutters brought me out of my trance. As the light gradually penetrated the room, I had this enormous desire to go out on our lanai. Our friends had left, and Chuck was outdoors opening the remaining shutters. Assuming the sumo wrestler position, I rose, leaning on my walker for support. I slowly opened the sliding door. What a delightful sight. I was greeted by a flock of ducks and ibises picking at the grass across the shimmering pond. A blue heron gracefully strolled by, and our three resident wood storks appeared, looking for an afternoon snack. Carefully sitting down, I noticed a black cormorant, wings spread open, soaking up the sun in our neighbor's yard. Such magnificent splendor, and more tears.

Chuck joined me and asked, "Darling would you like a snack or cold drink?"

"Nothing right now," I answered. "Just sit next to me please."

Pulling a high-backed chair beside me, he reached for my hand and brought it to his lips, something he does quite often during our day. I smiled. No words were spoken. We each were engaged in our own private thoughts, probably thinking the same thing in unison: we're home, we made it, and it's going to be okay. A few minutes later, Chuck leaned over and whispered, "I love you." *It doesn't get any better than this.*

19

It's the Little Things

LYING IN BED WATCHING THE fan blades whirl, I came to realize I was in my own bed. Sunlight filtered through the slatted blinds, revealing a new day, a fresh beginning. I had no idea what time it was, deliberately choosing not to make the effort to turn on my side to see the clock, while at the same time thinking it must be time for my IV therapy. Our bedroom door was closed, another sweet gesture by Chuck to not disturb my much-needed rest.

The phone rang. Chuck picked it up on the third ring. I was sitting on the edge of the bed when he tapped lightly on the bedroom door.

"Good Morning, Sugah," he said as he kissed me on my cheek. "It certainly is good to be home."

"Just fabulous to finally be able to sleep in the same bed with you again," I replied. "Who called?"

"Wrong number," he told me. "I think your fan club will wait a couple of days to let you get settled before they check in. Are you ready for breakfast? We'll start with an appetizer of Vancomycin!"

"Can we eat on the lanai? I know it's a bit humid, but I just want to take in all the beauty that surrounds our home. Just let me wash my face and brush my teeth first."

"Your wish is my command," he said, smiling.

I was amazed I didn't feel the medication going into my veins. It just does its thing until the bulb is empty. Settling in to being back in Sarasota, we had one less thing to worry about since the staff at Johns Hopkins had worked diligently to make arrangements with a company in Tampa to deliver my IV therapy supplies to our home.

We sat at the table on the lanai and Chuck said a prayer of thanks before we started breakfast. Non-mushy oatmeal with fresh blueberries and strawberries tasted delicious compared with the soupy variety they served me at the hospital. Actually, I really can't complain about the food I received at Hopkins. Most of it was very good with a nice variety to choose from. But then again, I had been a school teacher, used to school cafeteria delicacies!

Words seem inadequate to describe the unbelievable joy I felt as I sat next to Chuck and savored this simple, glorious moment together as we watched a solitary duck glide across the pond.

Today, and I expect for some time to come, I am a minimalist; not quite a Henry David Thoreau sitting alone in his stark, humble cabin near Walden Pond, but a woman who appreciates the little things, the ones we all take for granted as we race through the busy days of our busy lives.

Although I don't have much peripheral vision in my left eye, I was sure Chuck was watching me. I didn't look at him. It seemed, recently, that every time I did, the tears began to well and I could not close the flood gate. This triggered Chuck to go into his problem-solving mode, wanting to help, but becoming frustrated when I didn't have an explanation or didn't ask for anything. I want to say the root of my behavior is hormonal, but that would be inaccurate. I'm way past menopause and although I cry at "The Star-Spangled Banner," I'm usually more in control of my emotions. So soon after being home, I think my brain was just gradually absorbing the fact that I had made it through this far, my tumor was gone, and the future was brighter than I once thought.

Opening the bedroom door after yet another catnap, I glanced at our dining room table filled with piles of magazines and envelopes. Chuck must have sorted the mail while I was asleep. I found him at the computer in his art room.

"Hey, sleepyhead," he said, leaning over the walker to give me a hug.

"I just don't seem to have much energy lately," I said. "Or maybe it's my biological clock out of sync since we've been home."

"Don't worry about it," he told me. "I'm not at the top of my game either."

Each day I struggled, trying to regain my strength, faithfully doing my exercises, eating healthy, taking short evening walks with Chuck when I wasn't too tired. I remained focused on the *now,* not the *yesterday*, striving to meet my secret personal goal of making it to Gecko's Grill and Pub the next Sunday to join friends for the season opener between the Baltimore Ravens and the Kansas City Chiefs. It might have been a pipe dream, but I was determined. The "Ravens Southern Migration" is a large group of former Baltimoreans who get together each week to watch the game. Most Ravens games are not broadcast locally unless they are being televised nationally. Our group keeps growing and we just have a blast being with each other. I knew Chuck needed this as much as I did.

Sharing small household tasks was a challenge, but most days I was up for the test. I desperately wanted to help Chuck with some light housework to lighten the burden on him a bit. I figured out how to use my reacher to take laundry out of the washer, one piece or sock at a time, and drop it in the dryer. It was quite a lengthy chore, but for me a rewarding accomplishment. It seemed like every little action was an experience which brought me closer to recovery, pushed me forward, and kept me going.

My determination paid off. There was a standing ovation when we slowly walked into Gecko's and were greeted by thunderous cheers, emotional hugs, and encouraging words. Decked out in my purple scrubs and a black Ravens T-shirt, I was astounded by the outpouring from friends we had only met a few years ago when we first moved to Sarasota.

Jeanne whispered as she hugged me, "I knew you would be here. So glad to see you both." *How did she know that I was coming?* After an unsettling night, filled with anxious thoughts, increased pain, and several unsuccessful trips to the bathroom, I had my doubts…but I sure was glad I came through, achieved my goal, and could enjoy that rewarding day.

With Chuck's help, I gingerly maneuvered myself up onto the pillow he had placed on the high-top, hoping I didn't have to move again until the game was over. My mind wandered as I attempted to watch the game, catch up with friends, eat my favorite tuna wrap, taking it all in. For a month, the hospital had been my whole world. Other than phone calls and visits from my immediate family, the only people I had talked to were doctors, nurses, other staff, and a few patients. I had experienced a brief re-introduction to the outside world through the generosity and caring of extended family and wonderful friends before we had returned home. Looking around at the spirited crowd, I was reminded of just how far I had come. I knew there were still hurdles ahead, but I took the opportunity to bask in the joy of that "Raven-ous" moment.

20

Remembrance

DESPITE HAVING A FAIRLY DECENT night's sleep, I felt like a dishrag. I dragged myself into the bathroom. I hoped washing my face would make me feel more alert. I was having a hard time understanding my lack of energy. You would think the excitement of the previous day would have increased my stamina; instead, I think it drained me. *Did I push myself too hard to try to put some order back into our lives? Did I overdo it? Is my body trying to tell me to slow down a bit? Susan, stop this senseless chatter with yourself! It's counterproductive and unnecessary. You're making yourself crazy. You had a great time and if you're paying for it now, so be it. Today is a brand new day.* I splashed more cold water on my face, hoping it would jolt me into a better place.

I sat on the edge of my unmade bed, breathed deeply, and gathered my thoughts as I tried to refocus and restart my day. Alone in my silence, I had an urgent need to re-examine all that had happened since January, and to put things in perspective. Ironically, *Rosh Hashanah*, the Jewish New Year, would begin at sundown on Friday, only five days away. How appropriate that this holiday is also called *Yom HaZikaron*, the Day of Remembrance—a time to reflect on the happenings of the past year. I tried to relax as I let my mind travel back through the year and my recent journey.

The day-to-day routine and activities of the previous six months seemed like a blur, and except for a few delightful times with Chuck, family and friends, nothing seemed that memorable.

Are you serious, Susan? How could you forget Susie and Me Days, *with the last minute editing, rewriting and formatting to have it ready for publication at the end of the summer? How ironic and comical that you wrote a book about "memory" and then forgot about it?* I guess since my total focus had changed with the diagnosis of "chordoma" and the urgency it presented, the prior months seemed of little importance.

Finding something to wear to synagogue on Rosh Hashanah was challenging since most of my dress clothes had tight waistbands, not exactly the best fit when you are still swollen. Chuck was so patient as he brought out a variety of outfits, holding each one against me, trying to find something I thought would fit and be appropriate. In an effort to keep my spirits up, he was wacky and comical; he mismatched items, pranced around in blouses that only fit over his head, and cracked side-splitting jokes. He knew how much going to synagogue this year meant to me, and he was going out of his way to make it happen, even though he thought it may not be the best idea. He knew it would be tough for me physically, but that not going would be harder for me emotionally.

I was resolved that if nothing fit I was going to wear my black scrubs (black is always in) with a pretty colored top. Chuck wanted to buy something new, but I insisted he shouldn't waste money. I remembered a couple of suits in the back of the closet that were a little too big for me. Why I brought them when we moved to Florida is a mystery, but women never know when those unsightly extra pounds may reappear.

The red suit I chose to wear fit my mood and made a statement—I made it! *No lingering self-doubt or absorption for me today.* I was on an emotional high as I entered the synagogue leaning on my walker. Heads turned as friends and congregants acknowledged my presence, many surprised to see me. My friend,

Deborah, moved over so we could have an aisle seat and parked my walker behind the last pew. Rabbi Mishkin left the *bimah* (altar) and walked over to welcome me back and gave me a big hug. Our emotional reunion opened the flood gates and I was unable to keep the tears in check. Chuck handed me his handkerchief and somehow I got it together.

Nothing had changed in my synagogue, but somehow it seemed fresher, brighter, even more welcoming than before. *Or was it me? Was I different?* I believe having this life-changing experience did transform me, giving me a greater awareness and appreciation for the simple beauty that had always been there, but was often overlooked.

I sat during most of the morning service, only standing when the ark (where the Torahs are stored) was opened. I pulled myself up using the back of the pew in front of me. Traditional bowing for certain prayers wasn't an option, so I lowered my head in reverence. I felt renewed, delighting in the prayers and songs of my faith as I read from the *Mahzor,* the High Holiday Prayer Book. My heart was filled with silent prayers of thankfulness. As I often do during Sabbath services, I thumbed through the *Mahzor* looking for meaningful passages or psalms which spoke directly to me. I truly believe it was Divine intervention which helped me turn to Psalm 116, *God Heard My Cry and Saved Me.* Tears blurred my vision as I read:

I delight to know that God listens,
And hears my voice of supplication.
Because God is mindful of plea,
I will call upon God as long as I live.
The pangs of death encircled me,
The agony of the grave seized me,
Anguish and despair took hold of me.
Then I called upon the Lord:
"O Lord, save my life."

The Lord is gracious and beneficent,
Our God is compassionate.
The Lord protects the simple:
When I was brought low God saved me.

After two hours, I left synagogue tired but energized.

21

Tuesdays with Janet

S URPRISINGLY, WE DIDN'T HAVE TO wait very long before a nurse took us back to an examining room. It was ironic that my appointment with the infectious disease specialists coincided with a phone call from the Infusion Center in Tampa letting us know Medicare would no longer pay for my home IV therapy, but would pay for treatments at an infusion center.

A doctor wearing glasses and a green polo shirt with grey slacks shook our hands warmly.

"My partner is away this week, but will be back on Monday. We both have reviewed your discharge summary and the notes Dr. Thomas sent us from Johns Hopkins. How are you doing since you returned to Sarasota?"

How am I doing? Where do I start? And how much time do I have to respond? Be precise Susan, and brief.

"I'm okay," I said. "Each day brings new challenges after being away for so long. I tire easily. I'm still in a considerable amount of pain, but I'm focused on trying to gain a little more strength, do a little more each day, so maybe I can relieve my fabulous husband and caregiver of a couple of the responsibilities he has been handling since my surgery. I'm limited in what I can do since I can't bend. Dr. Wolinsky said it would take quite a long time before I would feel like myself again."

"With the extensive and complicated surgery you underwent, what you're relating is understandable. I would like to see your wound now, if you don't mind."

After a minute, he said, "You have a beautiful incision and it looks like it is healing well."

I replied, "Everyone who has looked at it was also impressed with Dr. Simmons' skill."

"We agree it would be in your best interest to change your IV therapy medication from Vancomycin intravenously every twelve hours to one dose of 350 mg IV Cubicin once a day. Our plan is to treat you for a period of four to six weeks. You will remain on your oral Ciproflaxin every twelve hours. You will need to come to our infusion center every day since your insurance will no longer pay for home IV therapy. Are you okay with that?"

Am I okay with this? Of course I am. Do I have another option? Hopkins told me my wound cultures grew a bunch of things that I can't pronounce or spell. And I want to get well, the sooner the better. Anything to take the unforeseeable financial burden off of us is fine with me. "What time should I be here tomorrow?" I asked.

The infusion center was an interesting place to say the least. Black leather reclining chairs with flip-side desks lined two adjoining rooms, mostly occupied by patients attached to IV lines that were dripping medications into their veins. A team of perky nurses juggled their time from one patient to another, scooting around on seats with rollers, getting up to get supplies, attending to each by changing IV bags, dressing wounds, giving explanations, or chatting to soothe occasional anxiety.

A nurse, or at least someone I thought was a nurse, pointed to a vacant chair and said she would be with me momentarily. As I waited, my eyes scanned the room and I noticed most patients were elderly. Many had a bandage on one of their extremities;

others, from the looks of their toenails, appeared as if they hadn't seen a podiatrist in years, and a few were sound asleep. Before I had a chance to empty the "to do" tote I brought, a dark-haired nurse pulled over a rolling stool, introducing herself as she sat down.

"Hello, I'm Karen, and I'll be working with you today. I've reviewed your chart, so I'm aware of what type of surgery you had at Johns Hopkins and the complications you had afterwards. So you know what to expect each day you come in, there's a sign-in sheet in our waiting room and someone will call you to come back to our infusion room. We try our best to keep to your scheduled time, but we never know how long it may take with other patients or if someone may need extra wound care, so I just wanted to let you know there could be some delays. You will probably get a chance to get to know all of our staff, since we work as a team, sharing responsibilities to meet the needs of all our patients entrusted to our care. Any questions?"

"Not at the moment."

"Let's get started then."

After wiping my pic line with an alcohol wipe, Karen flushed out the line with saline before hooking up my IV bag and starting the drip. She told me today's infusion may take a little longer, since she had the drip flowing at a slower speed than usual to see how well I tolerated things.

"Call me if you need me, okay?" she said.

The stack of thank-you notes I had planned to write lay idle on the small desktop attached to my chair. I had a difficult time focusing and getting my thoughts together. Glancing around the room, I realized there was a story and a history occupying every chair, some more complicated and serious than others, but all with the common result of needing some type of IV therapy. I tried reading the Prevention magazine I had brought, also to no avail.

As the Cubicin slowly dripped into my veins, my concentration was interrupted because of what was going on with my neighbor on my right. I tried not to stare. It's the first time I wished my peripheral vision in my right eye wasn't so sharp, so I wouldn't see the frightfully nauseating, oozing wound on the left leg of the gentleman next to me. His foot was variants of black, blue and purple, with only two thick trophic toenails. My first instinct was to reach for the sunglasses in my purse. Thinking that would be too obvious and show my disgust, I closed my eyes and settled back as if to take a nap. The next thing I knew, Karen was calling my name. As I came out of my stupor, I noticed the empty chair next to me. *Count your blessings, Susan*, I reminded myself.

A week had passed. A very tall, slim man, wearing khakis with a light blue button-down shirt and solid, darker blue tie pulled over a rolling stool and sat down in front of me. He extended his hand as he introduced himself with a warm smile. After chatting a bit about my case, he told me he would be following me, and to expect to have blood drawn once a week to see how I was progressing. Although I was trying to stay focused on what he had told me, I found it comical to watch this towering doctor navigate in such a small space, rolling between patients, straddling the stool with his long legs.

As he moved on to the next patient, I found it somewhat disconcerting to overhear my neighbor's case discussed in such detail. Unless you were deaf, it would be impossible not to pick up on what was being said. Where was one's privacy? I understood the rationale behind this policy and had signed a paper agreeing to it, but that didn't mean I liked it. To have each patient, most of whom were elderly, talk with the doctors in their private office, would take a lot of time, limiting the number of patients who could have treatments each day. This was not about the money, but more of a logistical strategy because the need for their services was so great. The supply and demand circumstances meant less-than-ideal scenarios, but I, for one, was grateful to be receiving treatments rather than sitting on a waiting list.

Chuck and I had established a pattern centered around my IV schedule. Including drive time, my treatments usually took two to three hours each day. Chuck was able to switch his gym membership to a location closer to the infusion center, allowing him to exercise while I had my treatment. Our dear friend, Janet, offered to be my chauffeur on Tuesdays, to give Chuck a well-deserved break.

I loved my *Tuesdays with Janet.* Some Tuesdays she would wait in the waiting room for me, reading or catching up on things on her IPhone. Other times she would drop me off and go over to the Manatee Art Center. Janet is a talented artist, whose paintings have been exhibited in solo and group exhibitions in galleries and cultural centers. Her use of vibrant colors and mixed media reflects her unique style, creating beautiful works which always convey a message.

Tuesdays meant we would have lunch at Demetrio's Pizza House, sharing a pizza and salad, and giving me the opportunity to have quality *girl talk* with a good friend. Not that I didn't enjoy my time with Chuck, but we were spending so much time together lately, we needed some respite from each other. I wanted him to start to pursue his own interests again, and hopefully get back to painting.

Despite my resolve, there were days when schlepping to therapy was a real hassle. Even though I knew it was a means to an end, this routine was really getting old. I made every effort to stay upbeat and focused. Some days it just didn't work.

I watched the fluid in my IV bag slowly empty. It was my last day of infusion therapy. My blood work looked good. Both physicians met me in one of the exam rooms, hopefully for the last time. They were pleased with my progress and didn't expect any foreseeable problems in the future. Another huge step forward. I was so grateful for this fabulous team and the nurses whose expertise and humor had gotten me through the past six weeks.

Chuck greeted me with a smile and open arms. As I fell into his embrace, both of us simultaneously sensed each other's joy. I was mindful of the penetrating stares from people in the waiting room. I didn't care. It was our moment. And just to raise a few more eyebrows, I kissed Chuck passionately. One couple applauded.

Later that evening we celebrated by having a picnic dinner on Lido Key Beach. The intense heat of the day had eased, and the light breeze of fresh Gulf air was invigorating. I sat on a pillow on a folding chair, wiggling my toes in the cool white sand, enjoying the endless repetitive pattern of gentle waves soaking the shore, and then receding. How comical it was to watch the antics of sandpipers as they frantically ran back and forth dodging the incoming tide. And how amazing it was to see a pelican make a strategic dive from high above to catch his unsuspecting dinner, or observe an occasional dolphin rise from the deep.

I had the sudden urge to walk on the beach with Chuck. Making sure the remnants of our dinner were well out of view of the hovering seagulls, we cautiously made our way to the shore and level ground. The coolness of the wet sand felt wonderful beneath my feet. Chuck nonchalantly put his arm around mine and gripped my hand for added support. There was something extraordinarily comforting about having Chuck beside me. He exuded an inner strength, a power that showed in his tender grasp as he held my hand.

We walked in silence as the sun slowly made its descent. Although he couldn't fully sense or understand the extent of the pain and discomfort I was in, Chuck didn't continually ask a lot of questions about how I was feeling, which to me was a blessing. Early in our marriage we made a pact to be candid and open with each other and not sugar-coat anything to make the other one feel better. I have to admit I occasionally didn't hold up my end of the bargain, and I suspect he may have slipped sometimes also.

Chuck was cognizant of how far we were going, knowing we had to retrace our steps. The sky was illuminated with rich tones of fuchsia, orange, and lavender as the sun crept behind the horizon. In a flash it was gone; a reminder this fabulous day was coming to a close. Chuck's gentle, tender kiss in the parking lot seemed like a natural ending to an enjoyable evening at the beach.

October 9

To all my supportive Family and Friends,

It's a little over two months since I had my surgery. I am certainly stronger and improving each day. Everything isn't back to normal just yet, and my neurosurgeon said it could take up to a year to fully recover from my extensive surgery.

It is so nice to be back in our home in paradise. Yesterday I completed my IV therapy. Hallelujah! I am getting out more, and even went to services for a couple of hours both days of Rosh Hashanah and for Yom Kippur. Yesterday was a real milestone for me. I drove to Publix grocery store with Chuck. Today I am going to CVS by myself. Life is good!

Chuck and I are planning a trip to Richmond to see his children and grandsons before we come to Baltimore for my MRI and two doctor's appointments. I'm really excited about it, since we didn't see the boys this summer and really miss doing things with them. We will be in Richmond four or five days and three days in Baltimore. Before we travel north we have a wedding on the beach at Treasure Island in Florida for friends of Scott and Bridget. Then they're coming to visit us for a few days. We have another wedding for Janet and Harvey's daughter when we return. Not sure how I'm going to do all this, but I'm happy to say that great things are happening for us. We appreciate every day and each other even more now.

Love to all,

Susan

22

A Sigh of Relief

I WAS NO STRANGER TO MRIs, but today neither the serene "Sounds of Acadia," the CD I brought with me to listen to, nor the raucous hammering and piercing sounds of being enclosed in Hopkins massive scanner could distract me from thinking about my tumor possibly returning. Words like "tend to grow back" and "dedifferential" were echoing in my head. *Breathe deeply Susan. It's not like you to get ahead of yourself. Concentrate on the beautiful, tranquil music of nature's symphony. Allow it to transport you to a more relaxed state.*

As I listened to the hypnotic cadence of waves rumbling against the ocean shoreline, I could feel the tension begin to leave me. I retraced the wonderful memories of our trip to Maine, of the splendor of Bar Harbor and the mystique of Acadia National Park. I remembered getting up at four in the morning to watch the sunrise on Cadillac Mountain, one of the first places in the United States to see the sunrise. I also recalled having breakfast sitting on the rocks overlooking Thunder Hole, hearing the deep roaring sound of waves crashing against the inlet as water shot forty feet in the air, sending spray skyward. The cliffs lining the rock-bound coast were majestic. I laughed inwardly, thinking about those soggy tuna wraps we ate at a pavilion deep within the park's magnificent forest. How much fun we had, taking an artist's studio walking tour, where Chuck conversed and learned techniques from local artists. We had afternoon tea at the Blue

Willow, and savored luscious late dinners as we watched sunsets over lobster boats dotting Bar Harbor.

Startled by the echo of a voice saying, "This last set will be about ten more minutes," I realized I had fallen asleep. I awakened still thinking of our time at the Blue Willow.

Serenaded by the
harmony of harp and flute –

I sit –
at an open window,
table covered
in tapestry cloth
with a pale rose vase,

sipping –
steamy mango-apple tea
from a delicate flowered pot
trimmed in bright gold,

feeling –
a fine salty mist,
the gentle warm breeze
brushing across my face,

watching –
the continuous pounding surf,
a lone seagull perched upon a post,
a shabby lobster boat heading home,

finding –
exceptional personal joy,
simplicity in this moment
at the Blue Willow,
Perkins Cove, Maine.

Dr. Wolinsky entered the exam room and closed the door behind him. His words, "Your MRI looks good," defused the internal apprehension that still lingered. I tried to be precise when answering his questions, knowing how valuable his time was. I had my list of bullet points I wanted to make as well as questions. With my long and complicated medical history, I always came prepared to all doctor's appointments.

I answered "yes" to completing my IV therapy, to making good progress, to no longer using the walker except for long distances, to still having a lot of pain, to having difficulty sleeping especially when turning, to becoming easily fatigued, and to faithfully doing my exercises to build my strength back. "Some days are better than others," I said to Dr. Wolinsky.

"I'm not on any prescription pain medications, and I only take liquid ibuprofen or Tylenol when I need to. It felt like Dr. Simmons didn't have enough skin to put me back together— something is causing constant pulling and hypersensitivity at the incision site. Lately, I've been getting these 'butt shocks' that can be quite intense. Thank goodness they don't last long, but they do happen frequently."

In his usual easygoing, confident tone, Dr. Wolinsky explained that besides having to sever nerves S4 and S5, he had to move many nerves and muscles to get to the tumor. Those nerves were stunned, and the shocks I felt were caused by the nerves regenerating. Dr. Wolinsky suggested I consult with a pain management specialist when I returned home.

I was so grateful I still had bowel and bladder function. My life would have been completely different if Dr. Wolinsky had to sever S2 and S3. Although it wasn't perfect, my plumbing still worked. I told Dr. Wolinsky I continued to have bowel issues, alternating between losing stool (I wear Tena underwear) and constipation, despite eating fruits and vegetables, taking Citracel twice daily, stool softeners, and my bran mixture. "My stool often gets stuck and can be quite painful, and I have to manually push it out."

"The S4 nerve is minimally involved with bowel function," Dr. Wolinsky said "It usually doesn't cause a problem. Obviously, in your case it has. As I emphasized before, the rectum is normally attached to the sacrum. In your case, a large part of your sacrum was removed which may be contributing to your bowel movement difficulties."

"I have an appointment with my gastroenterologist when I get back to Sarasota. I hope he has some solutions."

"Have you heard from Dr. Liebsch at Mass General yet?" he asked.

I told him I had not, and Dr. Wolinsky suggested I give him a call. He assured us that all my records had been sent to Dr. Liebsch, but knew he fastidiously reviews everything before contacting the patient.

"If there aren't any more questions, I'll see you again after you go to Boston. You can have Crystal set up your appointment. Make it around the next time you come to visit your family in Baltimore."

Both Chuck and I had been in awe of Dr. Wolinsky's knowledge, talents, and compassion. Before we left I asked him, "How does it make you feel when you know you just saved someone's life?"

"I'm usually thinking about how tired I am. I'm more concerned about the complications that may arise coming down the line than anything else." *What humility!*

Laura, Dr. Wolinsky's nurse practitioner and right hand assistant, approached us while we were standing in the narrow hallway waiting to make my next appointment. I was so glad she was in the Clinic at that time.

"I see you still have your pillow."

"Always. It's become a part of me. I feel like I'm sitting on two rocks most days.

"You look wonderful," she said, and gave me a big hug. "Sarasota must agree with you. I hope you feel as good as you look."

"I've been working at it. Some days it's not that easy."

We were struck by the kaleidoscope of vibrant fall colors—rich tones of red, orange, sienna, and yellow—which lined the highway as we drove towards our son's home. How I missed the beauty of autumn since moving to Florida, and its annual rituals of raking leaves, children gleefully jumping in the newly arranged piles, picking out that perfect pumpkin for Halloween, the taste of fresh squeezed apple cider, and the variety of homemade stuffed scarecrows and carved pumpkins peppering the neighborhood lawns. I did not miss, however, the October chill which had greeted our arrival, signaling that winter was not far behind.

Actually I was looking forward to a much calmer trip this time, only visiting with our children and grandsons and not trying to keep our usual crazy schedule of attempting to see as many relatives and friends in the limited amount of time we had when we came north. Due to my new normal, our pace had to be slower. Everyone understood and didn't press us.

Without any grandiose plans, the time spent with our family was actually more enjoyable, and everyone delighted in the simplicity of conversation, laughter, and shared memories—almost a lost art in this technology-centered, over-scheduled pace we Americans tend to keep. For me, just being with family was a gift.

The endless energy and uninhibited comments from our five grandsons, ages five to twelve, in Richmond, could keep anyone's spirits up. They were so eager to bring us up to date with all their latest school and sports activities, showing us everything from memorabilia from their summer trips, latest school work and projects, as well as the current books they were reading.

Three brothers had started "The Kids Reading Corporation," a special designated area in one of their bedrooms set aside for reading and keeping track of all the books they had read. How I laughed when I saw the banner they had proudly made hanging on their wall with a fictitious 800 number on it, just in case other kids wanted to get involved.

They were full of questions about my surgery, asking typically appropriate ones for their age and understanding. "Did they have to saw you open to get to the tumor? How big was it? How long did the operation take? Did it hurt? Was Papa there? How do you go to the bathroom if you are asleep? What happens if you wake up before the operation is over? How can you sit without a tail bone? What did the doctors do with your tailbone?" I jokingly thought–*Maybe they gave to the Museum of Natural History!*

They kept firing one question after the other, listening to the answer but eager to talk about their next one. I loved the animation in their eyes, their inquisitiveness, and the fact that they were even interested. I was honest with them and gave answers which I hoped were on their level. I knew how their parents "parent", being open and honest and not sugar-coating life's realities. When the inquisition was over, they all had to try out my foam pillow.

Our grandson, Charlie, and I needed private time together. He was nine and convinced it was his fault I had to have this operation. His flawed logic came from an experience one summer while we were at Hershey Park in Pennsylvania. We had ridden on the log flume together at least five times in a row. He knew I had fractured my coccyx sometime after that. None of my explanations seemed to satisfy him. With sad eyes he kept repeating, "But I know it's my fault."

As a young child he was curious about so many things and his questions were often challenging, showing maturity beyond his years. Making eye contact with him, I took both his hands in mine and said, "Charlie, this is truly not your fault. Papa and I didn't know a thing about bony tumors before going to the Mayo

Clinic. We talked to their doctors. We did some research on the Internet. We found out I was born with this. Even if I had never gone on the log flume with you, or gone twelve more times, it wouldn't have made any difference, because I had this before we got on the ride. I was born with this. I had it when I was a little girl, when I was a teenager, when I was a teacher, when I gave birth to Craig and Scott, and before I met Papa. Sometimes the cells that are in the tumor never grow and sometimes they do, but not very often. Mine did and it's very rare. No one knows when it started to grow or could have stopped it from happening."

"Could God?" he asked poignantly.

"I guess He could have, Charlie, but that wasn't in His plan for me."

Charlie looked away as if he had to think about that comment. "There's one other thing I want you to know," I said. "If I hadn't broken my tailbone and wasn't in so much pain, I might never have gone to the doctor and the tumor would have kept on growing, getting bigger and bigger, making it much harder for Dr. Wolinsky to remove it."

"Could you have died?" he asked.

"There was a small possibility if the cells inside the tumor had spread to other parts of my body, I might have. I had a test at the hospital before my surgery that showed my tumor was only in one spot and had not spread anywhere else."

Charlie's demeanor changed. His sad eyes were now bright as he eagerly asked, "Does that mean I helped save your life?"

"You had a lot to do with it." I replied.

"That's cool," he said.

Giving him a high five I said, "That's way cool, Charlie!"

155

23

Get Several Sheets of Paper

I WAS CHECKING MY EMAIL when the phone rang. "Is this Susan? This is Dr. Liebsch." I looked at the clock. It was quarter of nine on Wednesday night. *Unbelievable!* Dr. Liebsch asked me if my husband was home and if he could get on the other line. Unfortunately, Chuck was out with a friend, but I assured him I was ready to take notes and would relay anything he said when he returned. Dr. Liebsch suggested I get several sheets of paper.

Dr. Liebsch was delighted to hear I had completed my IV therapy and that I was making good progress. He said he had reviewed all the reports Dr. Wolinsky had sent him from Johns Hopkins, but wanted a little more information. He proceeded to tell me exactly what data and records he needed, specifically detailing how he wanted the material organized. The cover page was to include personal contact and insurance information, Social Security number, and patient identification number, which he gave me. Dr. Liebsch gave precise directions as to what should go on the left, the right, the top, and the bottom of each page.

Feverishly trying to keep up with his requirements to insure I wouldn't miss anything, I realized I was inventing my own shorthand, which I hoped I could decipher after we ended the conversation. Dr. Liebsch wanted a timeline of my chordoma history with each page to include dates, all physicians' contact information, what my pain scale was for each documentation, the prescribed treatment and recommendations, where tests and scans were done, and any personal comments I thought would be helpful.

It was the same involved format for my other medical history, starting from birth to the present. *He's got to be kidding. Who can remember back that far?* Dr. Liebsch's request list for the family history page was simpler, just wanting ages, whether they were deceased, and what their medical conditions were for both my maternal and paternal sides, my children included.

I was trying to remain focused, but this was overwhelming. I found myself playing catch-up, drawing arrows when additional needs were interjected, writing in the margins, using the front and back of each sheet, frantically trying to get all of it down. I realized there was a lull in the conversation. *Should I wait or say something? I can't believe there isn't a standardized form for recording this information with an enclosed cover letter explaining what information Dr. Liebsch wants and what format he wants each patient to use, which could be sent via mail or email. This seems a bit outdated, but I like this personal touch of being able to converse with your doctor prior to meeting him. It's certainly a rarity in this day and age.*

Dr. Liebsch also wanted the discs and written reports from any x-rays, MRIs, or CT scans. He suggested I send all of this documentation by certified mail, and told me his address at Massachusetts General's Proton Center.

"Do you have any questions, or is there anything you need clarified?" Dr. Liebsch asked.

"I think I have it all," I said, "but I'm sure I will need to go over these notes [five pages] several times so I have the layout correct. This will definitely be a challenge. I hope my recall is good enough to get the sequencing of events accurate, especially with my long medical history."

Then I asked about the schedule for my radiation treatments. "I will spend a great deal of time reviewing your information, so the sooner you can send everything to me, the sooner we can have you scheduled to come to Boston," he said. "In your case, when there is infection involved, I like to wait a month or two, to make sure there is no recurrence. Someone will be contacting you with your dates and pertinent information. I expect you will probably have between thirty-five and forty treatments." *Wow, that's at least seven weeks or more, with weekends. That certainly wasn't on my radar. I guess I was pretty naive when it comes to all this.*

"Will you need housing while in Boston?" he asked. *This is another "wow." I can't believe this world-renowned radiology oncologist is concerned about where we will stay in Boston. This speaks volumes about who he is.*

"As soon as we have you scheduled, someone will be in touch with you about MGH's accommodations in the Boston area."

I glanced up at the computer. It was nine-thirty. We had been on the phone for forty-five minutes. *No one is going to believe this. I hardly believe it myself.*

I spent the next week at my computer delving into my past medical history, with little regard for anything else on my schedule. My chordoma history was recent, occurring within the last four years, so I could easily formulate that timeline. I developed an accurate account of how I was finally diagnosed, and included current reports to support what had taken place. Then, I diligently researched and rummaged through a box of old medical records that were in the garage. Why I kept medical records from 1971 and schlepped them from Maryland to Florida is a real mystery! Did I have a premonition? Was it a "just in case" scenario? Or was it Divine intervention? It didn't matter. I was glad I had them, especially since my recall is not what it used to be, as my children will attest to.

My brain was on overload as I worked to put the puzzle pieces together to give Dr. Liebsch a clear depiction of my complicated history. He had told me on the phone that sometimes little things get overlooked which can be significant when looking at the total picture. Using Google to quickly find addresses was a blessing, particularly for physicians who had moved over the years.

Chuck had set up a card table in our computer/art room so I could sort my old records and keep the dates straight. He was so supportive; aware of the challenge I was facing, encouraging me to take breaks, and only interrupting for meals or to bring me a cup of hot tea or a snack. He took care of our home, most meals, and made sure I exercised by walking with me around our neighborhood after dinner every night.

I felt a rush of accomplishment and relief while standing in line in the small post office not far from our home. I almost didn't want to hand my package over to the clerk behind the counter, not wanting anything to happen to it and aware how items tend to get lost in the vast postal system.

November 12

Hi Fabulous Ladies,

Chuck and I are coming to Baltimore on December 3, so we can surprise Scott for his 30th birthday. Bridget is having a luncheon for the family on the 5th. Then we're heading for Richmond for an early Xmas with Chuck's family. We didn't get to spend time with one set of grandsons when we were in for my follow-up appointment in October, since our eldest grandson came down with the H1N1 virus, and we were on Tamiflu and quarantined in a hotel for three days. We're leaving Richmond on the 11th. We hope to see my crew one more time before we leave.

Soooooooooo, I was wondering if you can join me for a "Ladies Night Out" on Thursday, Dec. 3 for dinner— time and place TBA. Our time is so limited this trip, so I hope I get to see you.

Hope all is well with everyone.

Love, Susan

The green postcard, acknowledging my package had arrived at the Francis H. Burr Proton Center, came a week later. Now we just had to wait for our arrival date.

24

Where to stay?

A N EMAIL WAS IN MY inbox when we returned from our trip
north. I was scheduled to have a consultation with Dr. Liebsch
on February 22. My radiation treatments would begin March 1,
only one week later. There were several attachments detailing
what to expect during my treatments, along with a map of the
Massachusetts General Hospital's (MGH) campus, and a list of
accommodations that gave a courtesy discount to MGH patients.

Affordable housing in Boston was our top priority, so I started
reviewing that information first. Two no-fee facilities sponsored
by the American Cancer Society caught my eye—a Hope Lodge in
Worcester, forty-two miles from MGH, and another Hope Lodge
in Jamaica Plains, a little over four miles from the hospital. Both
were specifically for patients receiving cancer treatment who
lived at least forty miles from Boston. Both facilities required a
physician's referral.

A woman with a pleasant voice answered the phone, identifying
herself as Abby Losordo from the American Cancer Society. I told
her our arrival date and approximately how long we would be
in Boston. She informed me the Hope Lodge is only for patients
who actually are in treatment, so even if we met the eligibility
requirements and a room was available, we couldn't move in until
the day before my treatments started, which would be February 28.
Abby said, "The sooner you complete the paperwork, the earlier
I can check for availability. Sometimes availability is tricky since

patients don't always leave on their scheduled departing date. Please have Dr. Liebsch send me a referral as soon as possible."

Thank goodness Chuck had saved the travel and packing list we made for Hopkins on his laptop. He just tweaked the clothing section a bit to reflect that we were heading to Boston in the dead of winter, rather than to Baltimore during its hot, humid summer days.

The responses to my email letting family and friends know the dates for my treatments were amazing. We were blessed with a fabulous group of cheerleaders whose well wishes were reassuring and humbling. I made a few phone calls to a few "more seasoned" relatives who didn't have computers. My Aunt Roz said, "Suz, how can you even think about going to Boston in the winter? It's so bitter cold up there. Can't they schedule it for the spring?" I delicately told her that you don't have a choice. When they say come, you come. *No need to close the hurricane shutters for this trip!*

Dear Dr. D,

I wanted to let you know what has transpired since my last appointment with you for coccyx pain. At the end of June, I went to the Mayo Clinic in Jacksonville for a routine rheumatology appointment at the recommendations of my rheumatologist, Dr. Peter Holt, in Baltimore, and my internist, Dr. Gerald John, in Sarasota. I had a thorough evaluation, including blood work, x-rays, bone scan, an EMG, and an MRI. The MRI showed a sacral chordoma rising from the sacrum about the size of a baseball. A biopsy was performed to confirm the diagnosis.

I went to Johns Hopkins Hospital for a second opinion, and was operated on by Dr. Jean-Paul Wolinksy, who skillfully removed the tumor intact, preserving the S2 and

S3 nerves. Both radiologists at the Mayo Clinic and Johns Hopkins, as well as the orthopedic surgeon at Mayo and neurosurgeons at Hopkins, believe the perineural cyst that was diagnosed from an MRI done at your office last year, actually was a sacral chordoma. My chordoma had doubled in size since the original MRI. I know chordomas are very rare, but I wanted to bring this to your attention so it will be on your radar, in case another patient may present with these same complaints.

Sincerely,
Susan Garbett
CC: Dr. R
 Dr. F

Unexpectedly, I received a letter from Dr. D a few weeks later, stating he had reviewed my MRI with his radiologist and they both stood by their diagnosis of a perineural cyst. I was surprised I received a response, but Chuck and I believe they thought I was going to sue them, which wasn't my intention at all.

PART TWO

*Unexpected Warmth
in Boston's Chill*

25

"No worry lines and no wrinkles!"

OUR FLIGHT TO BOSTON VIA Atlanta was pleasantly uneventful. We were in and out of Logan Airport within fifteen minutes of landing; must be a record, especially on a Friday. We just love the charm of the Beacon House, a renovated old building for senior housing, in the historic Beacon Hill section of Boston. Our studio apartment has a full kitchen. We are so grateful MGH has two floors for their patients at a reasonable rate. We just love the character of this restored old building and we couldn't ask for a better neighborhood.

Chuck and I did a dry run to Mass General to see exactly where the four buildings are that we need to go to on Monday and Tuesday. We checked out places to eat, and found the building with a gym for Chuck to exercise while I have my treatment. We were also able to pre-register, which will be very helpful come Monday. The receptionist told us that Mondays are always "zoo-ie" at the Proton Center. Thank goodness for the warm boots and thermal socks and gloves Chuck bought me. The high today was 22. After lunch we went to CVS and Whole Foods, and somewhere between the two I lost my prescription sunglasses. I was so glad we had leftovers from dinner the night before, because we were exhausted.

We didn't realize how tired we were until the fire alarm sounded at seven-something the next morning. We jumped out of bed, threw on some clothes, grabbed our coats and rushed frantically down the stairs to evacuate. To our amazement, one man sat nonchalantly reading his newspaper in the lobby, and three Oriental ladies were in another room, dancing in circles around a large mahogany table, arms gracefully waving over their heads. No one seemed "alarmed". Just a test someone told us. How foolish we felt, standing there bundled up in our winter coats!

Today we walked around Beacon Hill, with its narrow gas lit streets and brick sidewalks. At times, maneuvering the steep hills and uneven sidewalks with protruding bricks was quite a challenge. Although brisk, the sun was bright as we strolled through the charming mix of Federal-style townhouses and fashionable shops and cafes. It was a perfect setting for a delightful afternoon. Tomorrow we meet with Dr. Liebsch.

There were only three chairs vacant in the adult waiting area at the Francis Burr Proton Center when we arrived. Chuck grabbed two seats while I waited to hand the receptionist, Paul, our completed forms. Feeling a bit apprehensive, I attempted to read as we waited to see Dr. Liebsch. I noticed a fashionably-dressed young woman walking out of the elevator holding the harness of what appeared to be a Seeing Eye dog. With the dog by her side, she approached the waiting area and called out my name. From my response, she walked over to us and extended her hand. "Hello Susan, I'm Abby Losordo from the American Cancer Society. So nice to meet you."

"Lovely to finally get to meet you Abby," I replied. "This is my husband, Chuck. We can't thank you enough for helping us get a room at the Hope Lodge. It has taken a huge burden off of us." We chatted a bit and she handed me a welcome packet from the American Cancer Society, along with her business card, and said to call her if we needed anything else. We watched Abby and her dog move on as she called the name of the next patient.

Over the years I have made many calls to physician's offices, hospitals, labs, and clinics. I often play mind games with myself when speaking with someone on the phone, mentally picturing how they may look, or how old they may be, only from their voice. Most of my imaginative descriptions are way off target after actually meeting the person, but every now and then I am surprisingly correct. It's probably a bit peculiar, but it gives me something to do when my call is put on hold. In Abby's case, I was pleasantly surprised.

It wasn't long before a woman wearing a white lab coat, with blond hair pulled back in a short ponytail at the nape of her neck, introduced herself as Kathy Selleck, Dr. Liebsch's nurse. Friendly and personable, she let us know she would be his liaison as she escorted us into a small exam room.

There was no need to try and imagine what Dr. Liebsch would look like as we waited for him to enter. I had done an extensive Internet search and his impressive bio included his picture. He received his PhD from the University of Munich, Germany, and his medical degree from the University of Munich Medical School. Dr. Liebsch had completed a residency at both Mallinckrodt Institute of Radiology at Washington University Hospital in St. Louis, Missouri, and the Mayo Clinic in Rochester, Minnesota.

Smiling, Dr. Liebsch introduced himself with a firm handshake and began discussing the sizable folder he had with him. He was all business, asking me questions, commenting on Dr. Wolinsky's skill in removing my tumor intact without severing the S2 and S3 nerves, and giving us detailed information on what his expectations and protocol would be during my time at Mass General. I liked that he always maintained eye contact with us, pausing several times to ask if we needed further explanation. He was exceptionally thorough and detailed, while showing his compassion and understanding toward both of us.

He explained I would have a combination of both photon and proton radiation treatments, and he would be determining the number of each to achieve the best outcome for me. He reiterated that chordomas tend to grow back and this is the best preventive method to keep that from happening.

I was surprised I was to have photon in combination with proton radiation.

The following helped me understand the difference between the two:

> Proton therapy is an advanced type of radiation treatment which allows supercharged protons to enter the body with a low dose of radiation, stop at the tumor site, conform to or "match" the tumor's shape, volume, or depth, and deposit the bulk of their cancer-fighting energy directly into the tumor, while sparing surrounding healthy tissue. This is especially important when treating areas near or within vital organs: lungs, tumors near the eye, brain or esophagus, and when treating cancers in children.
>
> With conventional radiation therapy, X-ray beams pass through both healthy and cancerous tissues, destroying everything in the path of the X-ray beam and damaging both cancerous tissues and surrounding healthy tissue. Consequently, physicians must limit the dosages of traditional radiation to minimize the harmful impact to healthy tissues near the tumor. (MD Anderson)

As with other types of radiation, proton therapy requires a treatment team, including a radiation oncologist, physicist, therapist, a dosimetrist, and a nurse. Never having heard of a dosimetrist, my research found out it is a health professional that designs radiation treatment plans, calculates dosages for medical radiation, and often operates radiation equipment.

Dr. Liebsch escorted us to where I was scheduled to have a CAT scan (computed tomography). After taking my picture for his file, he left while an IV was being inserted in my arm. I'm patient and I know I have small veins, but there is a limit to how many times a person can be "stuck" without complaining. Finally, on the third try it was a "go." I was just happy none of their misses blew a vein. Dr. Liebsch made sure I was precisely positioned for my scan and everything went smoothly after that.

The three of us returned to the exam room. In his thick German accent, Dr. Liebsch delicately asked if he could examine the incision on my buttocks. We were totally taken aback when he said, "Dr. Simmons did a wonderful job closing you up. There are no worry lines and no wrinkles!" All of us laughed hysterically, with Dr. Liebsch turning the reddest of all. Who knew he had such a dry sense of humor?

Dr. Liebsch asked if either of us had any other questions. I told him I was still having bowel issues, either losing stool or having it get stuck and manually had to push it out. He explained my bowel wasn't being supported by my sacrum any longer, and that it hadn't found a place to permanently rest yet. He felt with time, things should improve.

This is one amazing doctor, and I have seen a lot of physicians over the years. He made sure we were comfortable with what he had covered during our appointment, and then asked us if we knew where there were places to eat in the hospital. We told him we had a campus map, but to be of further help, he walked with us to the central corridor and directed us to the main cafeteria. He took time to expound on other places to eat and what they serve at each. *What doctor ever does this?*

February 25

Hi Everyone,

We met Dr. Liebsch last Monday and were very impressed. He spent the entire morning with us, reviewing my history in detail, asking many more questions, and staying with me through my CT scan. Unbelievable!! Then he spent another hour examining

me and letting us know what to expect from my treatments—
some fatigue and skin irritation at the treatment sight and
of course those rare worst-case scenarios. Dr. Liebsch is an
expert on chordomas, and told us sacral chordomas occur one
in two million people, not one million, and I was born with
this. This type of tumor tends to come back, so the proton beam
radiation treatments are mainly preventive. He's all business,
but his softer side comes out in his humor and gentle manner. I
had an MRI Monday afternoon and another type of CT scan on
Tuesday.

Thank goodness I was able to contact my former retinal
specialist in Baltimore, whose secretary promptly faxed a
release form to MGH's Radiology Department, stating the
titanium clip in my left eye is non-magnetic and there wasn't
any problem with me having an MRI. I couldn't convince them
of that fact, even though they had a copy of the MRI done at the
Mayo Clinic in June.

Wednesday we took the subway to the Hope Lodge. It is very
nice and we could tell that the design was well planned.
Bedroom and living room are larger than the Pavilion at
Hopkins, and there are many quiet areas for residents to relax
in. We were able to move in Friday, two days early, which gave
us time to get settled and be ready for another meeting with my
doctor for my test results, simulation, and my first radiation
treatment tomorrow.

Our address is:

Hope Lodge
125 South Huntington Avenue
Jamaica Plain, MA 02130, Room 305

Keep in touch and let me know what is happening with all of
you.

Love,

Susan and Chuck

26

A Home Away From Home

THE ASTRAZENECA HOPE LODGE CENTER in Boston has forty private guest suites, each with a bedroom with two beds, a sitting room, and bathroom. The common areas include courtyards, a library, a theater room, a game room for guests and their visitors, and a large meal preparation and dining area on the main floor. Each guest floor has a living room area with a flat-screen television, a laundry room, a computer area, and a quiet space by each stairwell for one to read or reflect. Guests who stay at the Hope Lodge are able to take advantage of the on-site resources of the American Cancer Society.

When people with similar situations are thrown together in a place where they never imagined they would be, the veil of privacy (for most) just naturally seems to lift. There was a story behind every guest's door. Some willingly shared their trials and tribulations, while others remained silent. Gratefully, there appeared to be an unwritten understanding that anything shared in conversation would remain safely within the confines of the Hope Lodge walls.

The oddest thing was, except for those who continually wore hats or scarfs to hide their hair loss from chemo, most of us looked just like anyone else you might pass on the street. Passersby never saw the havoc cancer had caused inside many of our bodies, or glimpsed the emotional and mental struggles we wrestled with.

Any trepidation about sharing a kitchen with other residents was unfounded. We were assigned to the "Daisy Kitchen," one of four kitchens, each located in a corner of the huge community dining area. Each was fully equipped with every kitchen item imaginable, with two enormous freezers and two refrigerators so each resident could have a shelf for their perishables and frozen items. Everyone was assigned a locking cabinet for staples and given a list of rules for residents to follow to keep the area clean and sanitary. All meals were expected to be eaten in the community dining room, mainly to keep the personal living areas clean. Eating together also provided an opportunity where patients and caregivers could come together to meet each other, share experiences, converse, relax, and draw strength from one another. It was an amazing space, a center where friendships were formed, support was given, and many events took place.

Our routine at the Hope Lodge revolved around my radiation schedule and whether the schedule for the Hope Lodge van coordinated with those times, so each day was a little different. The van made several daily trips between five of the top hospitals in Boston: Dana Farber, Brigham and Women's, Mass General, Boston Medical Center, and Beth Israel Deaconess. This service was truly a blessing for the guests at the Lodge and the only requirement was that you sign up the night before. If my radiation treatment didn't coincide with the van's schedule, we would take the subway, which had stops right across the street from the Hope Lodge and the hospital.

Acclimating to our new environment was easy. Bryan Harter, the Director, and Kate, the Assistant Director, and Brittany their Associate, were friendly, welcoming, and extremely helpful. Guests seemed to be in various stages of transition—some at the end of their treatments almost ready to leave, some just arriving, and others somewhere in the middle of their Boston journey—so faces were constantly changing.

Cliff, the guest-appointed "Mayor of Hope Lodge" and a stem cell patient, stepped into the role of greeter, tour guide, and master of the coffee maker, welcoming newcomers by telling them the ins and outs of their new home. Cliff and his sweet wife, Jean, certainly were experienced "Lodgers", having already been guests for two months before we arrived.

Most of our ten "Daisy Kitchenaires" and their caregivers were pleasant and approachable, but understandably, not all. A few were in the throes of chemotherapy, in different stages of physical turmoil and mental distress—not exactly the best conditions for gaiety and sociability.

For example, you almost never saw Linwood except for meals, and that was only because he had to eat in the community kitchen. He was a tall, thin man, who always wore a wool hat when he joined the group for meals. He chose to sit by himself at the counter, exchanging only a few words, not because he wasn't interested in being with other people, but because he really felt lousy. Being alone, Linwood would conjure up enough strength to come downstairs only because he knew he had to try to keep his strength up to face the next day's treatment. Not everyone understood his dilemma, and many residents thought he was being aloof and unfriendly. Chuck went out of his way to befriend him, trying to be understanding without being too pushy or overbearing. Some days Linwood was receptive to Chuck's overtures; at other times he was not. I was proud Chuck saw the need and stepped up to the plate.

Sharing a community kitchen for three meals each day with nine other patients and their caregivers took a real effort in patience, tolerance, and open-mindedness. At times it was a hub of activity as people tried to prepare their food without intruding on one another's space. Some folks were better at it than others. Since everyone had a different treatment schedule, it usually worked pretty well, except at dinner time, when everyone seemed to converge all at once in the same area.

Not every newcomer took time to become familiar with the kitchen rules, and others thought they pertained to everyone else, but not to them. Our dear Pearl, a "more seasoned" African-American woman who was the caregiver for her husband, Adley, shared her wisdom and kindness with everyone. Diplomatically, she made sure every person understood that the dishes had to be rinsed thoroughly before loading them in the dishwasher, and the counters cleaned, and the floor swept. She became the matriarch of the Daisy Kitchen, a lady of deep faith and tolerance—except when it came to people not taking responsibility for themselves and the health of others. We frequently found her unloading soiled dishes from the dishwasher, re-rinsing them as a precautionary measure as the rules stated.

One evening, as guests came down to prepare dinner, they were surprised to see every possible inch of counter surface in our kitchen covered with trays of meatballs, while Hawk, a pleasantly eccentric and a bit quirky guest, continued to hum away as he was preparing another batch of meatballs. Pearl's expression was priceless, while mine was not so understanding. Most of us decided to sit and chat at the tables and wait it out, hoping this meatball assembly line would be completed soon. I believe it was our curiosity which led to this choice more than our open-mindedness. *What is Hawk going to do with all those meatballs?* Watching this whole process unfold reminded me of the candy factory episode from "I Love Lucy," where Lucy and Ethel feverishly tried to keep up with the quick pace of the conveyor belt. *I'll probably dream about meatballs tonight!*

Our hunger won out over our patience, and Pearl elected herself as the go-between for the group. Whatever she said to Hawk had him repeatedly apologizing to us within minutes. He had been so involved with what he was doing, he simply lost track of time.

This is a perfect example of when the adage "don't judge a book by its cover" holds true. Later that evening, we found out

Hawk was the primary caregiver for four people in his family—his aging sickly parents, a mentally-challenged brother, and an elderly aunt—all of whom depended on him for almost all their daily needs. Although he lived in Massachusetts, he was very concerned that his cancer treatments in Boston would interfere with his responsibilities. Hawk explained that the meatballs would be frozen so he could take them with him on the weekends when he went home to his family "to do the pills and bills," as he put it.

So this unconventional guy—with his wide brimmed hat, flip-up sunglasses, fanny pack around his waist, and with binoculars, a camera, and money holder all hanging around his neck, looking more like he was going on a safari expedition rather than to a hospital for radiation—was really a hero.

One of the most rewarding bonuses encountered while staying at the Hope Lodge was the number of interesting people we met from all over the country, all with unique experiences, with the one common bond of having some form of cancer. I loved hearing the accents; those locals from the outskirts of "Bahston," to the thick ones from "New Yawk," to the deep southern drawl of folks from Virginia, Texas, Tennessee, Kentucky, Georgia, and the Carolinas, and me adding my hometown slang of "Bawlmer" (Baltimore).

Everyday interaction became an adventure as we greeted new arrivals and said farewell and good luck to those who were going home. Some people you hardly got to know because they were at the end of their treatment, or they had chosen to keep to themselves, while others you met were establishing friendships you knew would last long after they returned to their "old life."

Such was the case when we met Cindy and Barrie, a couple from upstate New York, who were approximately our age. Barrie was the patient and had previously spent time in Boston having his second major surgery at Brigham and Women's Hospital. They had been staying at the Hope Lodge in Worcester, Massachusetts, a charming nine-room guest house forty miles from Boston, before a room at the Hope Lodge in Jamaica Plain became available.

How lucky for Chuck and me they were assigned to our kitchen. We immediately hit it off, talking about our lives before "THE" diagnosis, sharing stories about our families, and getting to know each other through laughter and a budding friendship. As the days passed, we became closer, forming a bond that none of us expected to happen.

March 7

Hi All,

I had four photon radiation treatments last week and will start proton treatments tomorrow. Everything is going well so far. I lay face down with my head wedged in a raised pillow, while the techs position me. I breathe shallowly for about 15 minutes without moving, and then I'm finished for the day. I meet with Dr. Liebsch every Friday to discuss my case and to answer any of our questions. He's a real gem!

Chuck and I were able to get together and have dinner with my cousins, Arleen and Michael who live in New York. They were in Boston to hear their daughter, Tara, present at a palliative and hospice care conference, and to see her inducted as a fellow in both disciplines. It was great to be with loving family and catch up.

The weather was in the 50's this weekend and we walked to Coolidge Corner on Harvard Street, a neat area with small shops, restaurants, etc. Chuck found a church to go to and I found a conservative synagogue. Today we walked around Harvard Square and University in Cambridge. We're doing well on the subway, and find that people are really friendly and helpful when we ask for directions.

It's kind of weird, but every time we ride the subway the old Kingston Trio song about the MTA surfaces in my head:

But did he ever return?
No he never returned and his fate is still unlearned
He may ride forever 'neath the streets of Boston
He's the man who never returned.

Hope everyone has a good week.

Love,

Susan

27

A Powerful Gift

How naïve I was to think I could cook like I usually did at home. I had even brought plastic snack bags filled with spices, so I wouldn't have to buy expensive jars for only a pinch of this or that. Cindy looked at my collection and just roared with laughter. "When do your think you'll use all of those Susan? Especially the marjoram? We're all thinking 'simple and easy' here. What were you thinking?"

So "simple and easy" became already-prepared meals, baked this or that, ground "whatever" with all kinds of delectable sauces, carry-out for dinner, soup and sandwich for lunch, and the standards for breakfast. Chuck and I regularly had salads from the huge impressive salad bar at MGH either before or after my treatment. The Lodge van made weekly stops to both Stop and Shop and Trader Joe's. Also, Cindy and Barrie had their car and offered to take us shopping which was a blessing.

Hawk, being the generous and kind man that he was, frequently made food for other guests. One evening, Cindy and I found four gigantic cans of marinara sauce in our community cupboard and put together an Italian night for all four kitchens. Cindy, being a school cafeteria manager, made the spaghetti sauce, while I opened the cans. I had to laugh when she asked me for some of my spices. Each kitchen made their preferable type of pasta. I was able to get Stop and Shop to donate garlic bread for the occasion.

What a wonderful evening of food, friendship, and frolicking, topped off by Chuck and a few male singers attempting to sing their version of "That's Amoré." With arms outstretched to each side of their neighbor, everyone rocked from side to side, boisterously singing, "When the moon hits your eye, like a big pizza pie, that's Amoré..." We were having so much fun even without the vino (Hope Lodge rules), "cancer" was never mentioned. On another night, Cindy made vegetable soup and I made Greek pizzas.

Our hearts went out to guests and their caregivers who were having stem cell therapy to treat their type of cancer. Many were in clinical trials, having exhausted other more conventional cancer treatments. Most of these guests had to wear facemasks and rubber gloves whenever they left their apartment to protect them from infection—after a stem cell transplant, their immune systems were weakened from the treatments. They never ate food prepared by anyone at Hope Lodge. Many were forced to remain in their apartments a lot more than the rest of us, preventing them from participating in many of the activities and from sightseeing around Boston. It was necessary for them to have a private showing of a movie in the theater room. I remember Jean telling me how isolated and lonely she and Cliff often felt, living in such a controlled environment, missing a lot of the social life other people were enjoying.

I knew stem cell transplant involved an injection or infusion of healthy stem cells into the body to replace those stem cells which were diseased or damaged, but I did not know much more than that. I later learned that the procedure to replace healthy stem cells can also be known as a blood or bone marrow transplant, depending on the source of the stem cells. Stem cells can come from the bloodstream (peripheral blood), the umbilical cord blood of a newborn, or from bone marrow.

A physician makes recommendations depending on the set of circumstances and diagnosis as to whether a patient uses cells from their own body, from an identical twin, relative, or unrelated donor. If patients are not using their own cells, then a donor bank searches for the best possible match by taking DNA samples from both the patient and the donor, checking all twelve factors of the required criteria to get as close a match as possible. The closer the match is to 100%, the more likely the treatment will be successful.

Stem cell transplant is similar to a blood transfusion, where donated stem cells travel through a central line that is placed in a person's vein. Over a period of time, these cells begin to settle in the bone marrow and hopefully make new, healthy red and white blood cells and platelets. It appeared that our stem cell friends had a much harder road to travel than many of us at Hope Lodge.

Although there wasn't any formal written agreement, most people respected the confidentiality of others, and did not ask a lot of questions concerning diagnosis, treatment, or medical history. Most became good listeners if someone chose to talk about their cancer journey, but had the common sense to value people's privacy, even if they may have been a little inquisitive.

That was not the case with Darwin, a scientist who was from New Jersey. He asked a hundred questions of just about everyone, and personal ones that most of us thought were none of his business. Many people were caught off guard by his assertive overtures, not quite knowing how to respond to his unsettling and insensitive queries. He was persistent, determined to find out all the intimate details, the whys and wherefores concerning a person's cancer. His analytical, investigative mind was such a part of who he was, it never entered his thoughts that he was invading someone's privacy.

Darwin's thoughtlessness came to a head one day in the community kitchen. He had told Robert, a guest whose eye socket was damaged, distorted, and severely inflamed, that his disfigurement was disturbing to him and other people. Darwin tactlessly suggested that Robert and his wife eat their meals in their room, not in the dining room. Robert's wife, Frances, whose tears showed her distress, shared this troubling situation with

Chuck. She asked him if he could possibly intervene on their behalf. Chuck was appalled, and without hesitation told Frances he would have a talk with Darwin. He urged Frances and Robert to continue to have their meals in the community dining room with everyone else.

I was incensed when Chuck told me the story. I'm not a violent person, but I wanted to smack Darwin on the side of his head to knock some sense into him. How could anyone be so insensitive, especially since Darwin was receiving radiation for a tumor behind his own eye?

Chuck later took Darwin aside and firmly reminded him of the merits of common decency, compassion, and respect. Whatever Chuck said to him must have struck a chord, because Darwin apologized profusely to both parties after their conversation.

Actually, Darwin wasn't naturally mean-spirited or a deliberately malicious person, but his quizzical makeup was a part of his DNA and he just couldn't help himself from going overboard at times. Perhaps his incessant questioning of everyone helped him take his mind off his own problems, but he didn't have a clue that his words had caused Robert and Frances so much pain and anguish.

Thank goodness Darwin left Sharon alone. Her medical journey had been a roller coaster ride as she had tried to navigate through a maze of doctors in North Carolina before coming to Boston. She appeared strong, a real trooper, worrying more about being away from her young daughter for so long than the ordeal she was going through. Like others at Hope Lodge, the effects of radiation were quite visible on her face which appeared very red, almost like sunburn. I never knew what type of cancer she had; it really didn't matter. It was more about befriending and laughing with her, and supporting her when she was having a bad day. Years later, I found out Sharon had fibromyxoid sarcoma, a very rare cancer of the left sinus, resulting in the loss of her left sinus and upper pallet, and ultimately the loss of her left eye.

March 8

Hi All,

I had my first proton radiation treatment Monday, and it went well but was a bit intimidating even though I had seen a video about what to expect online before we came to MGH. Imagine a very large cavernous room, three stories high. Then imagine a platform on the second floor with a table that protrudes half way out into this ginormous open space. You can look down one story and up one story, and here you are lying face down in the middle. I was strapped in; weighted blankets were put over my shoulders and legs so I couldn't move. I was positioned correctly and a brass aperture designed especially for me was placed on my lower back in the specific area for my treatment. The techs leave the room and the table moves forward, like a gantry for a moon rocket, out over the void where you are surrounded by a 12-ton circular magnet (picture a room-sized CT scanner). The treatment begins. You don't feel anything, but you hear muffled sounds made by the machine as it goes through its programmed cycle. Monday, I could feel my heart racing, as I tried to remain calm and practice the shallow breathing that I'm supposed to do. Tuesday was a piece of cake, now that I know what to expect. Wednesday and Thursday were even better.

Tuesday I received a wonderful gift from the "Daughters of the King" from Chuck's church. These wonderful women crocheted a beautiful healing blanket especially for me. The passage on the card attached to the blanket read:

> *May the Lord bless you and keep you.*
>
> *May the Lord make his face to shine upon you and be gracious to you.*
>
> *May the Lord lift up his countenance upon you, and give you peace.*

These are the same words my father recited in Hebrew for almost fifty years, each time he blessed the congregation on holidays and festivals at our synagogue. As the tears flowed and I read this passage over, I felt my Dad's presence, letting me know that he was shining down on me and that everything was going to be OK. What a special moment this was for me and I am grateful to all these women that I don't even know, who took the time to make such a caring and compassionate gift.

I told the story about my healing blanket to Cindy, one of the guests at Hope Lodge who has become a dear friend. Her words to me were from her favorite quote:

> *There's no such thing as coincidences;*
>
> *It's just God's way of remaining anonymous.*

What a powerful quote!

Tuesday was a movie night at Hope Lodge with popcorn, and in between I had a massage given by a lovely volunteer masseuse.

It's been a great few days!

Love,

Susan

P.S. I can't say enough about the Hope Lodge and how fortunate Chuck and I feel to be able to stay here. We are meeting such wonderful people from all over the country, many who are having chemotherapy, radiation, or stem cell or bone marrow transplants. We are all cheerleaders for each other, which is really tremendous.

Hugs,

Susan

28

Generosity Abounds

THE TITLE OF A NEWSPAPER commentary I once read was, "What is happening to the America I once knew?" I've heard talk show hosts and so-called experts argue this topic on television and radio, while others prefer to give their opinion and analysis through blogs across the Internet. Many believe the changes are very troublesome, and caused by corporate greed and self-indulgence. They deplore our era of technology which has consumed us to the point where we text each other within the same room in our own homes; they lament that as Americans, we have lost our compassion and civility towards one another due to a "me first" attitude. This is not what Chuck and I have come to believe. All those naysayers and pessimists just need to spend a week at the Hope Lodge to witness the generosity of others whose volunteerism, donations, and sincere desire to make a difference in the lives of people they don't even know, is extraordinary.

Thanks to a seven million dollar donation from pharmaceutical company, AstraZeneca, and donations from philanthropists, organizations, foundations, three area hospitals, and from hundreds of individuals, the AstraZeneca Hope Lodge opened its doors in November, 2008, two years ahead of schedule. Donor names are etched on a large plaque adorning the lobby entrance, as a tribute to their commitment to expanding access to state-of-the-art treatment for cancer patients living outside the greater Boston area.

But the kindness of others goes way beyond any monetary amount. Businesses and corporations regularly donate coffee, tea, cleaning supplies, high-efficient laundry powder, popcorn, and other items guests may need or want. People often drop off tickets to the Boston Bruins ice hockey games, the Celtics basketball games, or the Red Sox baseball games. Interested guests put their names in a basket for a chance to win these tickets in a lottery. One woman planned an excursion and got tickets for many of us to an art show by the Harbor and another to the Museum of Fine Arts, which wasn't too far from Hope Lodge. Others volunteer their time and talent by playing music, giving massages, organizing game nights, cooking meals, sponsoring ice cream socials, decorating for different holidays, or helping with clean-up, organization, or landscaping. All of us were amazed at the outpouring of love, magnanimity, and support from complete strangers.

Frequently, notices were posted at the front desk as to what group would be coming and what event was being planned. You could hear the buzz around the community kitchen when we found out a group would be preparing dinner for everyone that night. For those who were exhausted or were feeling miserable, a provided dinner was a welcome gift, but it was also a much needed respite for those of us, patients and caregivers alike, who were tired of trying to come up with new and interesting easy meals every night.

Watching people's faces as they came off the elevator and approached the community kitchen was priceless. Most, like us, stopped dead in their tracks as they surveyed the spread that was before them. We were warmly greeted and told dinner would be served as soon as the majority of guests came down.

That night, a wonderful group of men and women transformed our community kitchen into a gourmet restaurant. Tables were draped in white cloths with black napkins, and a fancy, edible fruit arrangement adorned each table, individually made by one of the volunteers. Several baskets of flowers brightened the room. Tables were arranged in the back of the room to form a long buffet, lined with white china plates, baskets of silverware, a huge bowl of salad, assorted dressings, and several chafing dishes filled with roasted herbed chicken, beef tenderloin, long-grain wild rice, string beans almandine, and hot rolls. The center island held cheesecakes, assorted cakes, and brownies.

They were such a welcoming and friendly group, responsive to everyone's needs, offering to get us anything we wanted, and taking time to sit down with us and just chat. It was a fabulously memorable evening; a much needed "feel good" kind of night, where for a few hours the emphasis was on friendship, laughter, and gratitude, rather than on why we came to Boston.

All types of groups and organizations planned activities and events for the guests. Chuck and I enjoyed talking with the college students from various sororities and fraternities, finding out where they were from, about their families, and their goals and aspirations. It amazed me how focused most of them were, with many having a specific game plan for their future, so unlike me when I graduated from high school. Talking with them was uplifting, knowing most would be successful and make a difference when they graduated. Seeing their compassion and desire to help others amidst their hectic college schedules was refreshing. Their enthusiasm was contagious, their commitment a gift.

Others chose a different route to help out. One young girl sent an e-blast to her friends and family asking them to bake something to be donated to the people at Hope Lodge. In turn, her email was forwarded to their contacts, and the effort snowballed and generated so many scrumptious delicacies, the entire long island in the middle of the community kitchen was filled with sweets, some stacked on top of one another. It was unbelievable! Since there were way too many goodies for us to consume, some were frozen, and others were delivered to pediatric units at area children's hospitals.

Even our talented guests pitched in, providing wonderful experiences for those who chose to participate. Mary, who I remember always wore the most beautiful head scarves, sponsored a card-making evening, where guests and any visiting children or grandchildren were invited to participate in her art project. Brandon, a professional photographer, led several photography classes, which were very popular. No matter who came, or what they brought or did, all of the guests were grateful for their willingness to give of their time to help others.

March 18

Dear Family and Friends,

The most amazing thing happened yesterday as many of the Hope Lodge guests were chatting after breakfast. We see this man and woman along with a few staff members from Hope Lodge bringing in all these non-perishable groceries and staples, I mean boxes and boxes, piling them on the center island in the community kitchen for anyone to take. After inquiring, I found out that Bond Brothers, the company that constructed the building, regularly sponsors fundraisers to help raise money to continue the work of the Hope Lodge and help ease the financial burden on its guests. After losing their grandfather to cancer a few years ago, these wonderful people continue to help others.

The Hope Lodge runs solely on donations, and provides free lodging, transportation to and from five cancer centers, and amenities to forty cancer patients and their caregivers. The average stay for each guest is six weeks or more, saving each one approximately $7000. Chuck and I feel so privileged to be able to stay here.

I was so moved by the generosity and compassion of the Bond Brothers and so many others that I am asking if you might consider making a small donation to help out. Any amount would be appreciated by Hope Lodge and Chuck and me. Checks can be made out to The Astra Zeneca Hope Lodge and sent to:

AstraZeneca Hope Lodge
125 South Huntington Avenue
Boston, MA 02130

Thanks so much.

With love and blessings,

Susan

29

Bonding at Hope Lodge

THE DREARY, BONE-CHILLING WEATHER OF Boston was relentless, and we all wondered if spring would ever come. You could even see the gloom on the worried-looking, despondent faces of Bostonians who regularly rode the subway. No one smiled. Yet inside the Hope Lodge it continued to be warm and cheery, as friendships among cancer fighters were being formed.

Believe it or not, Chuck and I were actually having a great time at Hope Lodge, as were many others. Folks usually saw Chuck hopping from table to table, with coffee in hand, schmoozing and chatting with many of the guests, frequently saying his goodbyes to some or welcoming newcomers. Chuck had built a trust with a few of the more introverted guys who felt comfortable enough with him to share their inner thoughts and feelings. These breakthrough conversations happened occasionally when he was using the computer, and a guy using the computer next to him started talking. I was so delighted they reached out to him, because I knew Chuck could make a difference.

It seemed like we were constantly giving hugs and well-wishes to those leaving, and smiles and handshakes to those who just arrived. It was like a revolving door, a constant flux of people moving in and out of the Lodge. Not only were new patients arriving, but new caregivers also—friends and family members of long-term guests who were helping out for a short period of time. It wasn't unusual to see a new face in the kitchen and hear,

"I'm here for so and so. I'll be here for two weeks. I'm replacing so and so who left this morning."

Bonds were being formed; connections were being made. Chuck and I were becoming very close with Cindy and Barrie. Jean and Cliff from Kentucky, Gail and Dick from Georgia, and Karen and Mike from Tennessee became our southern circle of friends.

You would often see us moving tables so we could share dinner together. Everyone got to know each other quickly as we talked about ourselves, our families, jobs, past lives, and our dreams. There was laughter, there was joy, and there was gladness. We delighted in just being with one another, lifting up those who were having a bad day, reaching out whenever we could, celebrating small and big successes.

Once in a while, our kidding unintentionally felt inappropriate, almost insensitive, as someone suddenly became silent or their eyes became glassy. How wonderful it was to see someone intuitively place a reassuring hand over that person's, or see an arm reach around their shoulder. And yet with all the individual drama that was happening, you rarely heard any self-pity. *Was all this joy real or pretense? Were our smiles forced? Were our conversations consciously elusive? Was our closeness an illusion, a way of coping? Or were we fooling ourselves into believing everything would be okay, and that most of us would have good outcomes? I wish I knew.*

Often joining us were Mindy and her dad, Steve, who came from San Antonio, Texas. Mindy was a vibrant, energetic, thirty-something year old high school English teacher, and mother of three young children. Her smile was contagious; her blue eyes sparkled, her pixie hairstyle fit her personality. She bounced in and out of our community kitchen at a brisk pace we were all envious of. Except for a hacking cough, no one suspected she had such a serious condition—fourth-stage melanoma—and was in her sixth or seventh clinical trial. Her father had come to support her, since her husband and mother were taking care of her three children back home.

Another spirited duo were Ellie, a tall, striking seventeen-year-old with long black hair, and her youthful-looking mother, Flora, who came from Sacramento, California. Ellie told us she had complained of back and leg pains for a few years before her physician found a chordoma while doing a test for scoliosis. He told Ellie her spine would have collapsed in a matter of weeks had it not been found. She had emergency surgery a few days after her diagnosis and spent several grueling months in a body cast. She lightheartedly said, "I used to be such a wimp!"

Ellie became the third member of the unofficial *Chordoma Club*, a loosely formed group of women who shared the same diagnosis and were all under the fabulous care of Dr. Norbert Liebsch. Our stories were different, as were the locations of our tumors. Gail had a cervical chordoma, Ellie a lumbar, and mine was a sacral. During our time at Hope Lodge, we added two more women, a young mother, also a patient of Dr. Liebsch, and later, a woman my age who was having proton beam radiation to hopefully shrink her tumor before her surgery.

How I loved those early mornings at Hope Lodge—that new day feeling, hearing what now had become familiar voices, the rattle of pots and dishes being taken out of cabinets, and the bustle of others who were also beginning their day. It was exhilarating to think that this day could bring a new adventure, a new opportunity, as I mentally marked off the passing of another day on my internal calendar.

I would frequently find people sitting at the island reading the newspaper. You would usually find Steve working diligently on his laptop computer, or talking on his cell phone, trying to keep abreast of his business back in Texas.

As usual, Rebecca was already seated in "her chair." She was a thin blond from South Carolina who had stayed at the Lodge many times. Rebecca had politely claimed sole ownership of a particular chair, and there she remained most of the time except when she was having treatment. None of us could understand how anyone could sit that long in one spot and never move. But that was her thing, and everyone respected Rebecca and her chair.

Carol and Bill were a delightful couple from New York, with a wonderful sense of humor. Carol, the caregiver for Bill who was in treatment, was a diabetic who regularly took insulin, yet ate some kind of gooey dessert with every meal, including breakfast. I tried not to be judgmental, but many of us thought Carol and Bill went out sightseeing just to find the best bakeries around the city to satisfy her sweet cravings. Yet no one was upset when they brought back goodies to share with the rest of us.

The counter in the Daisy Kitchen, like the three others, became another center for conversation and camaraderie. Over my ritual morning bowl of oatmeal with some type of fruit, I watched folks conversing, sharing snippets of happenings from back home, or the details of what they were doing on a particular day. It was comical to see folks come down to make breakfast, in various stages of dress—a few still in their pajamas, others dressed but not fully awake, and still others wide-eyed and ready to conquer their day.

We all enjoyed listening to Pearl, with her astute commentaries sprinkled with a dash of humor and wisdom, as we watched her husband, Adley, automatically respond to her endless directions.

I always looked forward to seeing Cindy. She brightened my day, with her quick wit and insight. I was disappointed when she and Barrie weren't there, when they had already left for his very early treatment at Dana Farber. Those who overslept had just enough time to down a glass of juice or coffee, and grab a muffin or protein bar before the van left. They never realized what they missed in those early hours each morning.

The Hope Lodge van drivers, George and Brian, were special people. Their approach to the job went way beyond the countless trips they made back and forth to hospitals. They were experienced drivers able to maneuver through Boston's heavy, bottle-necked traffic and the congestion at drop-off points at hospitals. Like all the staff at Hope Lodge, they were patient, but they also became our psychologists, social workers, and cheerleaders, offering physical assistance as well as levity during our rides. Occasionally, if there weren't any more people scheduled to be picked up, they would take the scenic route home and show us a few of the sights around Boston, pointing out the non-touristy places to see.

There was a more tranquil atmosphere throughout Hope Lodge on Saturdays and Sundays. Those who lived within a reasonable driving distance usually went home and returned late Sunday night or early Monday morning.

I savored those quiet, less hectic times. I could read more and catch up on my writing, which had been put on the back burner during my arduous medical journey. I was working on a few rewrites for my book, *Susie and Me Days: Joy in the Shadow of Dementia,* a candid and intimate account of my relationship with my father as we journeyed through Alzheimer's and vascular dementia.

Sitting at the computer, feeling the keys under my fingers once again, was invigorating. As I wrote, I could almost hear "my words" cheering me on, as sentences became paragraphs and new pages developed, an internal message talking to me saying, "You're almost there!"

Since there were fewer people at Hope Lodge on weekends, it was easier to catch up on laundry rather than trying to use the washers and dryers that were constantly busy during the week. This chore was another one of the many routines of communal living that required patience and tolerance. Considerate guests would either move their laundry from the washer to the dryer, or remove their dried items within a reasonable time frame. Others would thoughtlessly leave either their wet clothes or the dried ones in the machines, tying them up for hours, not caring how it affected other guests. That really ticked me off as it did other people. You would sometimes see piles of wet clothes or stacks of dry ones plopped on the laundry table waiting for their callous owner to retrieve them. One time, I became quite upset when my clothes were missing from both the washer and dryer. I couldn't imagine anyone taking them. Panic set in until I realized I got off the elevator on the wrong floor.

Weekends also gave people an opportunity to sightsee around this magnificent city, explore its history, and enjoy many of its wonderful restaurants. We were grateful we had enough energy to do a little sightseeing. Other guests weren't as fortunate, only going out occasionally for short periods of time. Still others had side effects from treatment that kept them from any outings.

No matter where we went, my tempurpedic pillow went with me. I jokingly told Chuck we should Velcro it to my butt, since he frequently had to retrieve it from all sorts of places due to my absent-mindedness.

Walking in the freezing weather was not my thing, although I had no choice when it came to my treatments. Chuck and I chose indoor venues, anticipating warmer weather would be approaching shortly.

Although it was quite a trek getting to Columbia Point in the Dorchester neighborhood of Boston, The John Fitzgerald Kennedy Presidential Library and Museum was well worth the trip. For us, it was a stroll back in time that was still fresh in our minds. We had been teenagers when a young senator from Massachusetts became the thirty-fifth President of the United States. There was so much to observe, to read and learn about, it was impossible to take it all in. There were exhibits about JFK's campaigns, the Kennedy Family, his White House years, his briefing room, the Space Race, the Cuban Missile Crisis, the Civil Rights Movement, and of course, that fateful day in November, 1963, when he was assassinated.

Watching people of all backgrounds, especially young children who were learning about the President for the first time, sit behind JFK's desk was moving. It was a nostalgic day as we remembered a time when life seemed a lot simpler, less hectic, and talked about how it was "back then."

Another time, we took the subway to the Cambridge Side Galleria with Cindy and Barrie just for a change of pace. Even though it had the same stores as most other big suburban malls, it still felt wonderful to look at the store displays, browse a few shops, enjoy lunch at the Cheesecake Factory, and do something "normal" for a change.

On the one sunny day when the temperature climbed into the low sixties, we donned our tennis shoes and took full advantage of this gift from Mother Nature. We attempted to walk the Freedom Trail, the 2.5-mile-long, mostly brick path which runs through downtown Boston that leads to sixteen historical sites. Knowing we couldn't possibly see everything in one day, we took our time, choosing to stop at places we both were interested in. A history buff, Chuck especially enjoyed Paul Revere's Home, the Old North Church which had been used to signal the arrival of the British during the American Revolution, and King's Chapel, where British soldiers who were sent to America to enforce British laws had been housed. Of course, being an avid reader, he loved browsing inside the Old Corner Bookstore where Nathaniel Hawthorne, Charles Dickens, Ralph Waldo Emerson, and Harriet Beecher Stowe had often visited. I loved touring the Boston Latin School, the oldest public school in America, founded in 1635, where John Hancock, Samuel Adams and Benjamin Franklin had attended.

The area around Faneuil Hall was filled with people who were also taking advantage of the weather. Bright sunshine made it seem warmer than the temperature registering on the bank tower indicated. Who would have thought we could sit outside to enjoy lunch in Boston during March? Inside the hall, we browsed the market stalls on the first floor, realizing we were in the same place where colonists had met to organize protests against the Sugar Act, Stamp Act, Townshend Act, and eventually hatched the idea for the Boston Tea Party.

The desire to climb to the top of the Bunker Hill Monument, a tribute to one of the major battles in the Revolutionary War, was put on hold for another excursion at another time. We were exhausted. Both of us fell asleep on the subway back to Hope Lodge.

30

Amazing Technology

*Remember that beyond any clouds, the sun
is still shining. Meet each challenge and
give it all you've got. Count your blessings.
Climb your ladders and have some nice long
talks with your wishing stars.*

*Be strong and patient. Be gentle and wise.
Do every positive thing you can possibly do.*

*And believe in happy endings
because you are the author*

of the story

of your life.

—Douglas Pagels

THIS INSPIRATIONAL REFLECTION FROM DOUGLAS Pagels' book,
100 Things to Remember...and One Thing to Never Forget,
is one of my favorites. It's a gentle, yet powerful reminder that
we have choices in our lives, even when obstacles and burdens

are harsh, even when we are struggling; we still have the ability to take control and work to help ourselves.

I remember when I was first diagnosed. "The Fear" was enormous, the "what-ifs" overwhelming. I was determined not to let them swallow me up and consume me. Instead, I chose to embrace the news as a natural part of my journey, because I was *the author of the story of my life.* Was the fear there? Of course. Was it a challenge to keep it from surfacing? Yes. I gave "The Fear" time to do its thing, and then I used it to motivate me and push me forward, to do research, to gain knowledge, and to hopefully make appropriate choices. It was easier for me to remain strong and take actions in spite of fear since I was fortunate to have a loving, reassuring husband and a fabulous support network of family and friends.

I was breezing through my radiation treatments. They had become routine, except when my schedule was changed because the cyclotron was out of order. I had an advantage; my tumor had been removed intact. It was gone. My radiation treatments were only a preventive deterrent to keep the tumor from growing back.

Other people at Hope Lodge weren't as blessed. Some were having radiation to try to shrink the tumor before surgery, others because their surgery wasn't as successful as mine. For some, their cancers had returned, and a few had to endure radiation along with chemotherapy, a double whammy. I learned if you were getting proton beam radiation to your head, you had to wear a special, white, waffle-looking immobilization mask, formed precisely for each patient's face. I remember Carolyn telling me how claustrophobic she became when her mask was placed over her face the first time. "Just hearing them securely clamping down my mask, I felt like I couldn't breathe, which wasn't the case at all. It was still frightening. Being out there on that narrow table in the middle of this vast space, all kinds of unnerving things popped into my head."

I was grateful my treatment didn't require a mask. Each day I would walk past racks of various-sized masks and brass apertures which I later learned are brass blocks, tailor-made specifically for each patient. Each had an opening through which the radiation beam passed. The purpose of any type of immobilization device, whether for the head or any other diseased body part, was to minimize any movement by the patient, ensuring that the radiation beam only targeted the diseased tissue.

I had excellent teams at both the Proton Center and the Cox Building. Chuck and I met fascinating people from all over the world while waiting for my name to be called for treatment. I enjoyed waiting in the nearby children's area at the Proton Center because it gave me the opportunity to converse with the children, read them a story, sing along with the guitarist who came periodically, or help them with a puzzle. Although I have been retired for a long time, I guess that kindergarten teacher thing really never leaves you, and being with the kids became a diversion for all of us.

What you can accept in adults, is really hard to accept in children; so young, so innocent, so full of life, battling some really tough diseases. Their energy and resilience amazed me. You would see them come off the elevator with their parents and often with other siblings, dressed as princesses, superman, or whatever they felt like being on any particular day; some shy, some chatty, others clinging to their Mom or Dad.

Paul, the receptionist, was a real softy when it came to the kids. His banter, humor, and friendly, approachable manner made their time in the waiting area enjoyable. You would see them try to sneak behind Paul's desk to find the drawer with his candy stash, which he was happy to share with them, with their parent's permission. Fridays were extra special, when, after their treatment, each child and their sisters and brothers were able to pick a gift from the "Treasure Room." Thanks to the generosity of individuals and companies, this room was filled with toys, games, and kid-friendly accessories for all ages. What joy it was to see them as they proudly walked out to the waiting room, all smiles with their "loot."

It was great to see Abby and her seeing-eye dog at the Proton Center, although I was never sure how much she could see of us. Always dressed to the nines, she was an inspiration. Chuck and I enjoyed talking with her, but her time was limited because of the number of patients she had to connect with. I also looked forward to talking with Dr. Liebsch's nurse, Kathy, usually before or after my treatments. Compassion just radiated from her, which made her an amazing nurse. She was friendly, and so in touch with her patients, a perfect fit for the job. Her sense of humor some days had me in stiches. Kathy never seemed to get rattled by the hectic pace or sudden changes in the schedule at the Proton Center. You could ask her anything, and no question was too absurd. If your question wasn't in her realm of expertise, she would find the answer for you.

Kathy said her mom was showing some signs of memory loss, and often asked me questions about strategies to help her deal with the reality they both were facing. Even though I had become a support group facilitator for the Florida Gulf Coast Chapter of the Alzheimer's Association and continued to educate myself, I was still far from being an expert. I always felt Kathy's medical knowledge and experience as a nurse was far superior to my layman's background. Maybe having too much information put her at a disadvantage, especially when the personal, emotional piece entered into the picture.

Kathy was the point person when appointments were cancelled because of some glitch with the cyclotron. She was the calm in the midst of chaos, the steady rock of assurance. Sometimes when my time slot for proton radiation had been cancelled, they would squeeze me in for photon radiation that day, and a few times I didn't have any treatment at all.

Chuck and I signed up for a lecture by Ethan Cascio on the history of proton beam radiation therapy offered by MGH. Cascio had spent the past twenty-six years developing proton therapy as a revolutionary new science, first as a collaborative effort with the Harvard Cyclotron Laboratory (HCL) and MGH. At HCL he became the Operations Manager of the lab, responsible for the radiation effects program. At the Burr Center, he established and continues to manage the Radiation Test Program, providing clinical physics and engineering support for the program.

Listening to him, I realized he probably had given this program hundreds of times, yet even after all these years he still presented his information with the same enthusiasm as a young boy opening his first toy train. His discussion was fascinating; the photos imbedded in his presentation slides were captivating. It was a real eye-opener for Chuck and me, and everyone else who attended. I would like to say I understood all the technical terminology, but that wasn't the case. Having worked with technology for Bell Atlantic and then Verizon for thirty-five years, Chuck's comprehension was definitely far better than mine.

As articulate as Ethan Cascio's presentation was, my understanding of this complicated technology was still limited. To gain a better understanding of how proton beam radiation works, I consulted the following website:

http://neurosurgery.mgh.harvard.edu/ProtonBeam/ NPTCbrochure.pdf

For clarity, the Northeast Proton Therapy Center was renamed The Francis H. Burr Proton Therapy Center in November 2005.

> The Northeast Proton Therapy Center (NPTC), located on the main hospital campus of the Massachusetts General Hospital (MGH), represents the forefront of technological advancement in radiation therapy. The construction of the facility was jointly funded by the MGH and the National Cancer Institute

to meet the increasing medical demand for high precision radiation therapy provided by proton therapy. The program builds on more than forty years of pioneering work and experience gained by MGH physicians, physicists, and clinical support personnel at Harvard University's Cyclotron Laboratory where more than nine thousand patients were treated with proton therapy from 1961 to its closing in 2002.

At the NPTC, protons (charged particles) are accelerated with a large magnetic field in a machine called a cyclotron. Large magnets help guide the proton beam to three treatment rooms. Two of the treatment rooms incorporate 110-Ton gantries. These 3-story-high gantries can be rotated to aim the proton beam from various directions. In the gantry rooms patients lie on robotic beds that can be adjusted for precise alignment of targets contained throughout the body. The third treatment room contains two specialized "beamlines". The first beamline is specially designed to treat lesions contained in the eye. The second beamline is dedicated to high precision stereotactic treatments within the head.

The role of radiation therapy is to irradiate disease area while sparing adjacent normal tissues. If patients weren't immobilized, it would be necessary to treat a margin which reflects the motion of the diseased target. This would unnecessarily treat normal tissues surrounding the diseased area. This is especially important when using a high precision approach such as proton therapy. The immobilization specialist understands the treatment requirements so as to customize an appropriate device to be used for

both the pretreatment imaging, such as planning
CT as well as the treatments.

Since most of us who attended this presentation were on some type of delay or postponement in our treatment that day as a result of the cyclotron being down for repair, Cascio's presentation was expanded to include pictures of what it is like to be physically inside this amazing technology. The huge cyclotron's cavity needs to be opened before any examination, cleaning or repair can take place. Once opened there is barely enough space to move around, yet two experts must complete their meticulous work inside, wearing white sterile uniforms, caps, and shoe covers. Their job is extremely tedious, performed either bent over or lying down, since no one could possibly stand up. *How do they do this for hours upon hours, while systematically assessing and wiping down every inch of this life-saving equipment?*

One slide reminded me of a replica of the gigantic hamburger that used to be at the Playland at McDonald's during the 80's when my sons were little. Kids could crawl in from the bottom, climb up to reach its middle, and end up in a round, enclosed space encircled with bars, similar to the small space inside the cyclotron. Don't ask me why I thought of this. It probably had something to do with my kid-like desire to be in there with them, knowing full well I couldn't fit. Not that I ever want to actually be inside a cyclotron—just the thought of it makes me claustrophobic.

Schedule delays didn't happen too often, and Chuck and I didn't mind the inconvenience. We had already concluded that we would have to remain in Boston longer than anticipated. How fortunate we were to be in a place in our lives where a long stay in Boston wouldn't cause too much difficulty for us. Others weren't as blessed.

March 17

Hi All,

Scheduling has been crazy since the proton machine has been down for three days. I wasn't able to have treatment on Tuesday, but was rescheduled for photon radiation yesterday and today. In the middle of my treatment today the photon machine went down, so they switched me to another room. When they call you about changes, you leave everything and go.

Even though I bring something to read or do while waiting for my treatments, time tends to move slowly. In my boredom I wrote this poem for my Proton Radiation Team.

Precision Healing

Lying face down—
head wedged in a horseshoe-shaped pillow
arms raised overhead
focused on shallow breathing

Picturing—
a stream of invisible proton particles
penetrating my body
with precise accuracy,
beaming rays of healing
guided by gifted physicians,
extraordinary technology....

Radiating new hope, within me again.

I see Dr. Liebsch after treatment on Fridays. The Proton Center has to replace a twelve ton magnet beginning 3/26-4/19 by knocking out a wall and hoisting it by crane through the ceiling. They will only be running 2 of the 3 rooms on those dates from 7 AM to 8 PM, so who knows when my treatments will be scheduled. The children definitely come first thing in the morning, because they have to fast because they need to be sedated so they can't move during the procedure.

Please let us know what's been happening with you.

Love to all,

Susan and Chuck

31

That Look

YOU COULD BE SITTING IN the kitchen, looking for a book in the library, or standing waiting for the elevator, when you noticed a guest returning from whatever medical treatment or appointment they had that day. And you saw that look—that subdued, solemn face, the one that instinctively told you their news wasn't good. My first impulse was to give them a hug. My second told me not to invade their private anguish. My third was to silently pray, asking God for their successful outcome and to help me choose the right words if they decided they wanted to talk.

Many times I had to bite my tongue to remain silent, remembering to just listen. I was reminded of the perceptive book I once read, *Don't Sing Songs to a Heavy Heart,* by Kenneth C. Haugk. With great insight, the author described the feelings of a person who is ill, disappointed, disheartened, or sorrowful; someone who is experiencing some kind of anguish, misfortune, adversity or trouble. Haugk wrote about the superficial "sunny" cheeriness we often unintentionally display when someone is experiencing a "heavy heart." We tend to put the "I" in our conversations—"…when I had…," or, "…when something like that happened to me," instead of being more sensitive to their needs, letting our compassion and understanding focus totally on the person. I've learned that thoughtful silence may be the best communication in some instances. I once saw a plaque in the garden at Arden Courts, a memory care facility in Sarasota that read:

Love heals and comes in many forms—
the greatest of which may be silence.

When faced with these types of situations, I try to remember Haugk's advice on *what to say* and *what not to say or do*. I am getting better at it, but for me, it's still a work in progress.

Other days were much better, even joyous. Once, as Chuck and I were leaving Hope Lodge with an umbrella in hand, we saw a taxi pull up in the driveway. Joan got out and ran over and hugged me with such force I thought she would knock me over. "I have great news," she said as she backed away. "I'm cancer free. Can you believe it?" She then proceeded to pull off her cap and threw it in the air in celebration, reminding me of the intro to the Mary Tyler Moore Show.

Together, Chuck and I said, "How wonderful! We couldn't be happier for you." I picked up her cap which was getting wet from the light mist that had begun, handed it back, and said, "You might want to keep this as a memento of your successful journey and accomplishment. You may even want to have it bronzed!" We stood there in the drizzle, laughing, as our tears mingled with the raindrops trickling down our faces.

As the days and weeks passed, a few acquaintances blossomed into what we thought might become lasting friendships. Some people never made any attempt to connect with anyone, choosing solitude over camaraderie. I respected their decision, even though I truly believed everyone needed someone to bond with to help them get through their journey.

At times, people who sat with us didn't want to be engaged. They sat in what I would call a wandering silence, fading in and out of conversation, pretending to be interested in the small talk going on around them, their thoughts in a different place. *Were they just tired from an exhausting day? Had their optimism begun to fade? Were they carrying some heavy news from home? Were they just eager for their trial or ordeal to be over so they would know one way or another if their treatment had been successful? Or was this Hope Lodge experience just an illusion of closeness because of our circumstances?*

Nothing raised someone's spirit more than a visit from their family back home. The community kitchen became more alive, more interesting as we met guests' spouses, children and/or grandchildren. Their presence was a welcome change from the daily routine and monotony some of us were feeling after being at the Hope Lodge for so long. We were able to put a face with the names of family members that had already become familiar. Chuck and I relished our time spent with Karen and Mike's nieces and nephews, Pearl and Adley's son and grandsons, Cindy and Barrie's son, daughter-in-law and grandchildren, and Mindy's mother, husband, and three young children.

Most of us enjoyed watching the children's boundless energy and uninhibited behavior, listening to their unrestrained conversations, their questioning, and insatiable curiosity. Other people retreated to their rooms, not pleased with the extra noise and antics from kids just being kids. I was happy for those whose families were able to come, but sometimes I became melancholy, missing our own children and grandsons even more.

32

A Delightful Surprise

IT WAS UNUSUAL TO HAVE radiation on a Saturday, but a call came late one Friday night which told us the cyclotron was down again, and my photon treatment at the Cox Building was rescheduled for seven the next morning. Dawn came way too quickly that day, but our early subway trip to MGH was highlighted by a breathtaking sky with its distinct striations of color which followed us. As the sun emerged, the murky gray heavens brightened to cobalt blue, patches of dark crimson changed to reddish pink, and a deep orange blossomed into a golden yellow.

Surprisingly, I finished my radiation pretty quickly, thanking the staff for giving up their weekend so patients wouldn't fall too far behind with their treatments. While seated in the waiting area for Chuck to come back from the gym, I noticed colorful, handmade, twelve-inch material squares that were draped on a wire high above the receptionist's desk. From their simplicity and amateurish lettering, they appeared to have been created by children. Why I never noticed them before baffled me, but I became engrossed not only in their bold primary and neon-colored designs, but in the beauty of their messages: "Stay strong"; "You're not alone"; "God loves me"; "One Day at a Time"; "You can kick cancer's butt"; "Nothing is impossible"; "I'm still me, even without hair."

As my eyes scanned the length of the pennants, I was drawn to the square that had no written phrase, just two small hands pointing inwardly, thumbs touching, index and middle fingers slightly separated from the ring and pinky fingers, and the name "Sarah" signed in the lower right corner. Those tiny hands, simplistically arranged like the symbol for the Priestly Blessing spoke to me. *Is this the work of a Jewish child? Was her father a Kohen (priest), a descendant from Aaron the High Priest, who in biblical times blessed the Israelites on Holy Days and festivals, and whose tradition continues in some synagogues today? Was this Sarah's way of speaking to God, asking Him to bless her with a good outcome as she battles her cancer? Or was this Divine intervention since my father was a Kohen and my Hebrew name is Sarah?*

At that moment I saw my Dad standing at the altar, blessing our congregation in my synagogue in Baltimore. As the tears came, I felt his presence, letting me know he was walking along with me.

A man wearing a Red Sox T-shirt interrupted my thoughts as he announced to everyone what a glorious day it was outside. His enthusiasm sparked my desire to see for myself how truly "glorious" a day it was.

Later, as I walked across the campus, I felt the refreshing warmth of the sun. The tips of a few crocuses were just beginning to poke out of what used to be frozen ground. Several barren trees appeared to have new buds, signifying that spring was not far away. I spied an unoccupied bench, sat down, and shed my jacket as I called Chuck to let him know where to meet me. My call went immediately to voice mail, and I wondered if he had remembered to turn on his phone. Then I had an urgent desire to call my children. I had a nice long conversation with Craig, but Scott did not answer.

Either Chuck was engaged in a super-duper workout, or he never received my message. I was content to just sit and watch people, many in short sleeves and shorts, as they walked or jogged pass. After finishing three more chapters in the book I was reading, I felt my phone vibrate. It was Chuck telling me he was on his way.

"It's too nice a day to pass up," he said as he bent over to give me a quick kiss. "Instead of heading back to Hope Lodge, let's go somewhere. Any ideas?"

"Mindy and Lance went to the Historic North End for their anniversary," I replied. "She said there are tons of Italian restaurants to enjoy. I know how you love Italian food."

"Sounds great," he said. "You know I have no willpower when it comes to Italian. Hope I can figure out how we can get there on the subway."

We walked through Christopher Columbus Park heading towards Hanover Street, where we found oodles of restaurant and café choices. Chuck took my hand as we walked along, appreciating the old architecture, breathing in the wonderful smell of fresh baked bread, stopping occasionally to check out menus or gaze in the windows of the small shops. There wasn't much conversation between us, each immersed in private thought, relishing this time together and this gorgeous day.

My phone vibrated while we were having lunch and I saw it was Scott. Chuck nodded, confirming that I should take the call. I answered the phone and walked to the back of the restaurant where there weren't any patrons.

"I saw you called, Mom," he answered. "What's up?"

"Just wanted hear your voice. I miss you," I said. "What's going on with you?"

"Bridget and I are running some errands. We may go to the movies later. What are you guys doing?"

"I had radiation early this morning. It's a surprisingly warmer day here, so we're having lunch in a little Italian place in the North End."

We didn't talk long, just long enough to find out about his week and a few newsy happenings from Baltimore. Sometimes

Scott can be chatty if he made the phone call, and other times he seems pre-occupied. It doesn't matter; it was that maternal instinct to check in with my children once a week, even if they were adults or too busy to pick up the phone.

When I returned to our table, I saw my eggplant parmesan was still steaming, and looked way too hot to eat. I filled Chuck in on my conversation with Scott, and started to eat my salad. Only a few minutes passed when my phone vibrated again and Bridget's name came up.

"I just wanted to say hello, but Scott hung up before I had a chance to talk to you. How are things? Scott said you were doing well and at a restaurant for lunch in Little Italy. Which one are you at? I wonder if it's the same one I went to when I was in Boston."

"I have no idea what the name of this place is, but the food is delicious."

"Well, I don't want your food to get too cold, so I'll call you back later."

Again, I attempted to eat my meal when the phone vibrated for the third time, and indicated Scott was calling again. I may call in "twos," but not Scott, so I picked it up. "Mom, I wanted to surprise you, but you weren't at Hope Lodge when I got there, and now the two of you are in some restaurant in the North End. I'm in a cab, so would you please find out the name and the address, so I can find you?"

It took a moment for his words to register, to realize that he was here in Boston. When it did, I jumped up and ran out through an open street-level window, patrons staring at me like I was some kind of nut. "Hang on, Scott." Looking up I told him we were at the Florentine Café. "What street Mom?" I had to ask a passerby the name of the street. "Hanover Street…I don't have an address, but I'll go back in and ask. "Never mind, Mom. I see you."

I looked across the street and there was Scott getting out of a cab. As he waited for the light to change so he could cross, it took all my composure not to dodge the cars to get to him first. But when he approached, I grabbed him, my tears dampening his polo shirt. "Take it easy Mom; I didn't pack a lot of shirts."

By now Chuck was outside standing there with my pocketbook on his shoulder. He apologized for not remembering which weekend Scott was coming and causing him to go on a wild goose chase trying to find us. Chuck told him the couch in our apartment was still available. I was so excited. Again, I was a little slow on the uptake, but suddenly realized Chuck had known all about this surprise. Then I realized Bridget wasn't with Scott, and found out she was still in Maryland taking a class at Hood College for her Master's degree. Her call had been just a ploy to find out where we were.

Scott was embarrassed when we went back into the restaurant and I introduced him to our waiter, the owner, and a few patrons near our table who wondered what happened to us. He was starving, so he ordered while our waiter removed our plates to warm them in the microwave. I kept touching Scott, just making sure this was all real. I was beaming, and had a grin so big everyone in the restaurant knew how happy I was.

After lunch, we headed back to Jamaica Plain where we gave Scott a tour of Hope Lodge, proudly introducing him to the weekend staff and some of the friends we had made. After he retrieved his duffle bag from the front desk and we put the Italian pastries we had bought earlier into the refrigerator, we three hopped on the subway heading to Harvard Square. The streets in Cambridge were filled with crowds of people enjoying some street entertainment, shopping, and like us, trying to figure out which restaurant to go to for dinner.

With a forty-minute wait at the Border Café on Church Street, Chuck offered to wait for a table while Scott and I took off for Harvard University's campus. *This is just like him, always thinking of me, and wanting to give Scott and me some bonding time by ourselves.*

The engraving on one of the entrance pillars read, "Established in 1636," making Harvard the oldest institution of higher education in the United States. The buildings were just what you would expect—stately Ivy League structures of traditional red brick architecture, planned around well-manicured grassy areas. I relished our leisurely stroll together through Harvard's campus, and delighted in this rare opportunity to spend one-on-one time with my son.

March 20

Dear Fabulous Friends and Family,

Today was full of surprises, with a last minute, unscheduled Saturday radiation treatment, a spectacular relatively warm day for Boston, and a mind-blowing unexpected visit from my son, Scott. I was overwhelmed when I saw him.

We spent the afternoon at Harvard Square. Scott and I toured the campus while Chuck graciously waited for a table at a crowded Mexican cantina. Sunday we toured Fenway Baseball Park, guided by a seventy-five year old gentleman, who was the most animated, passionate and humorous tour guide you can imagine. His "shtick" was filled with detailed stories, anecdotes, and tidbits about his beloved "Bah-ston" Red Sox. I enjoyed our friendly back and forth teasing as I chided him with stories about my beloved Orioles.

We were able to sit near the "Green Mon-sta" (Monster), only a stone's throw from the famous 32 foot 2 inch high wall that towers over left field. Originally built of wood in 1912, it burned down with much of the park in 1934. The current wall, built of plastic, was assembled in 1976. Actually despite its name, the wall wasn't painted green until 1947. It's amazing— with all the latest technology and jumbotron TV screens in other stadiums, Fenway still has two scoreboard operators who manually update the scoreboard. It was so cool to step inside the Monster and see the thousands of players' autographs left behind over the years. Reportedly, Babe Ruth's autograph is somewhere. We didn't find it.

Our plans to tour the Samuel Adams' Brewery on Monday were cancelled after I received a call asking me if we could be at the Proton Center within the hour. Scott went with us and we had lunch together before he had to leave for Logan Airport.

It was a fabulous weekend!

Hugs to all,

Susan

33

The Dream

THE WEATHER IN BOSTON WAS certainly unpredictable. After five days of cold and torrential rain, the sun finally came out Monday and the temps have been in the high 60's. Chuck and I have done a lot of walking around the pond across from Hope Lodge and through the small downtown area of Jamaica Plain. How wonderful it was to see robins, budding trees and sprouting crocuses, jonquils, and tulips during our walks, all harbingers of spring. The gas grills and furniture were set up on the outdoor porch at Hope Lodge, another sign that the seasons were changing.

We had two special student groups from Northeastern and Boston Universities come to spend time with the guests at Hope Lodge. One group celebrated St. Patrick's Day with delicious Irish stew and shamrock-shaped cookies, and the other made matzah ball soup for Passover and Easter cookies. On another occasion we enjoyed an ice cream social and game night sponsored by relatives of one of the guests.

It was a little more than a week before the Easter holiday, and surprisingly nothing was being planned at Hope Lodge. Cindy and I knew those who were able would be going home, but we wanted to do something to make it special for those who remained. We put out heads together and discussed our ideas with the Lodge staff. They told us that someone had already dropped a ham off from Trader Joe's.

Sign-up sheets went up in all four kitchens, asking people to make a side dish or dessert from any of those listed for our holiday meal. It was wonderful to see how quickly people responded. A few people who didn't cook but wanted to participate, gave us money to use for whatever we needed.

Once the process started, things moved fairly quickly. Stop and Shop gave us a gift certificate and one kitchen offered to make a turkey. We had money to buy a few specialty items and some holiday decorations from the Dollar Tree. Cindy insisted we buy an Easter Paschal Lamb, sculpted from butter, a symbol of spring and a tradition in her son-in-law's family and for many Catholics of Polish, Russian, and Slovenian descent. Being Jewish and never having tasted ham in my life, Cindy gladly took charge of that preparation.

All this groundwork was happening at the same time I was preparing for the holiday of Passover, an eight-day festival commemorating the emancipation and Exodus of the Israelites from slavery in Egypt over three thousand years ago. Getting ready for Passover was always involved since no bread could be eaten, only *matzah* (unleavened bread). Separate dishes, utensils, and pots were used for cooking, and the house was cleaned so that it was free of any *chometz* (bread products). It took some ingenuity and creativity to observe Passover at Hope Lodge. I wasn't able to prepare the specialty foods I usually did for the holiday, but I was able to purchase many Kosher for Passover staples from area grocery stores. My meals consisted of lots of salads, fruit, hard-boiled eggs, jarred gefilte fish, packaged deli, and matzah with cream cheese, eaten on paper plates using plastic ware. Since I was a child, I have always loved this holiday, so I didn't mind the extra work.

I knew I was truly going to miss being with my family. It was a tradition on my father's side to join together for the first Seder, a family ritual that has taken place every year for almost a century. We always read from the *Haggadah,* which retells the story of the liberation of the Israelites from their enslavement in Egypt. We would enjoy a wonderful holiday meal, and cherish our time together, using it to catch up with our ever-growing family which we may not see during the rest of the year. My father led our Seder for as long as I can remember, until his short-term memory failed him and the beginning of Alzheimer's surfaced. I was glad that my sons and daughters-in-law would be at the family gathering to represent me and keep this time-honored tradition.

Although the weather was miserable and pouring, Chuck and I were able to enjoy both Seders at the Hillel House at Northeastern University. The first night was packed with students, many who forgot to RSVP that they were coming. Adjustments had to be made to accommodate the extra students, so we enjoyed first Seder on a pool table covered with a Hanukkah tablecloth. It's customary for the youngest child to recite the "Four Questions," asking, "Why is this night different from all other nights?" It was quite comical when the student leader asked all the freshmen to stand and say them together. These "home away from home" Seders were different, but really fabulous and delicious. It was our conversations with the students, however, which were the highlight of the evening.

Easter arrived two days later. The center island in the community kitchen was filled with beautifully displayed platters of several types of potatoes, string beans, asparagus, zucchini, and a variety of casseroles. There were huge bowls of salad and cut-up fruit, and luscious, mouth-watering cakes and cookies.

I was overwhelmed by Steve and Mindy's thoughtfulness and generosity when they presented me with a package containing two Kosher-for-Passover cooked chickens and a pan of brownies. They had walked to the kosher deli so I would have something special to eat, since I was still observing the Passover holiday.

Before our meal, I asked if anyone would like to join in for a non-denominational community prayer I had written. We formed a circle around the center island, and with hands joined and many heads bowed, I read:

> At this annual remembrance of miracles, we join together as a family in gratefulness—for the bounties of the season, for each other, for our fabulous Boston hospitals, for the expertise of physicians and other medical personnel, for amazing technology, and for the compassion and support received here at the Hope Lodge. Although we are far away from family and friends, we keep them close at heart knowing they are a part of us each day. Give us strength and comfort as we face each new challenge. We pray that all of us, through Your guidance and love, will have good outcomes, and hopefully one day there will be a world without cancer.

What a beautiful afternoon and evening of joy, friendship, and laughter it was. As I was feasting on my chicken, I spotted a couple standing in the entrance to the community kitchen. After finding out they were new guests, I asked them to join us for dinner. They were astonished by the invitation. I told Rose and Larry, "When you walk in the door, you're family." Rose joined us while Larry went upstairs to get some much needed rest, since he had an early morning test the next day. Before Rose sat down, we overheard her phone conversation telling whomever, "You won't believe what just happened!"

Many people did not want the festivities to end after dinner and gathered in the library/music room. Pat, a guest who ran a music school in Miami, played the piano. Joining her in song was her niece Michelle, who had come from Malaysia to care for her, along with Pearl and Chuck. Others in the room sang along. Pat graciously took requests. There were a few hymns, and a breathtaking and humbling rendition of "Ave Maria." We sang a few favorites like "Easter Parade" and "Here Comes Peter Cottontail." Remembering all the words was a challenge for most, and a bit comical, but my rendition of "Here Comes Peter Matzah Ball" had everyone laughing.

The back doors that led to a beautiful garden-like setting were opened, since the room had become quite warm. I glanced outside and saw Mindy sitting alone on a bench with her back to us, cellphone by her ear, immersed in solitude, most likely talking to her children back in Texas. At times, she talked openly about her cancer with a few people she felt close to, sharing details about her life, her journey, and her sadness from being so far away from her family.

Mindy wrote often on her CaringBridge page, an Internet site which offers free personalized websites to people facing serious medical conditions, hospitalization, or undergoing medical treatment. This service allows family members and friends to receive reliable information via a single website, and eliminates the need to place and receive numerous telephone calls. Mindy's posts were candid, descriptive, intimate accounts of her challenges, and the physical, emotional and financial burdens of her disease. They were frequently spattered with humor and sarcasm. She consistently reminded readers of the importance of using sunscreen.

As we were about to head up to our room, a Hispanic man in his early twenties from California who was there with his wife, stopped Cindy and me and told us, "This was the best Easter I ever had." We were thrilled.

Before I left, I saw Mindy, still sitting alone as it was beginning to grow dark.

34

Patience!

Even though there were abundant diversions to keep us occupied and entertained, we were still counting the days until we could return home. The trek back and forth to MGH was getting old, the routine at Hope Lodge tiresome, and a couple of people were getting on our nerves.

After dinner one evening, I heard Darwin drilling young Ellie with question after question about her medical history and chordoma surgery. He had been doing quite well with respecting people's privacy, but I guess his curiosity got the better of him. It wasn't my finest moment either. Listening to him, I had a sudden urge to leave Hope Lodge and get some fresh air.

On my way to the front door, I bumped into Cindy and Barrie coming off the elevator. They had jackets on and I asked them where they were going. "We're going for ice cream." Cindy said.

"Can I please come?" I pleaded. "I need to get out of here. Darwin is driving me up the wall!"

"You grab Chuck and some jackets and we'll get the car and meet you out front," Barrie told me.

Who knew a trip for ice cream at J. P. Licks could be so entertaining? The cool, melting sensations of vanilla snicker doodle on my tongue woke my senses and put me in a better frame of mind, as did our delightful conversation. But it was my dear husband who had us in stitches. Chuck had found a book he had been searching for and wanted to read for many years, just sitting on a shelf in the ice cream shop, of all places. He was beside himself with joy from finding *Winter, a Novel of a Berlin Family,* by Len Deighton, published in 1987. His comments were priceless. We thought he was going to have an orgasm when the manager told him he could keep the book. The more he talked, the funnier he got until the three of us couldn't stop laughing. Barrie had often affectionately called me "Suzi Q" and Chuck, "Chuckles"—tonight Chuckles really lived up to his name!

A few days later, a visit from Craig and Sonel really boosted our morale. Even though we had stayed connected by phone, it was so joyful to see them in person. Of course I gave them the tour of Hope Lodge, proudly introducing them to other people as we made our way around. After seeing the facility first-hand, they thought the Lodge was much nicer than my email and phone conversations had described. They were impressed with how many free amenities were included.

Sonel and Craig were staying in a Starwood hotel in Cambridge, since our room wouldn't accommodate two more people. My treatments were back on schedule which left more time to sightsee with them. We started our tour of Boston by boarding the "Duck," an authentic World War II amphibious landing vehicle that had been renovated for sightseeing. We cruised by all the places that make Boston the "City of Firsts" with its rich history. Our tour was enhanced by the interesting little-known facts and tidbits told to us by an animated and enthusiastic "ConDUCKtor."

After my treatment the next day, we met them at Cheers in Beacon Hill, the original Boston pub that inspired the setting for the television show "Cheers", an American sitcom that ran for eleven years beginning in 1982—the place "where everyone knows your name." We walked through Boston Common, the oldest park in the country. Of course we didn't cover the almost fifty acres, but just savored the beauty of the budding spring. They both wanted to visit Harvard University's campus, so we did the Square thing again for a third time. Before they left for Baltimore, we took the subway and had lunch at the Prudential Center, a complex of several buildings featuring many distinctive shops and restaurants, bordered by upscale hotels.

It's always hard to say good-bye to our children, especially since we live in Florida and they live in Maryland and Virginia. It was much easier this time since we were planning to visit the whole crew after we left Boston, before heading back home to Sarasota.

April 8

Hi Everyone,

Having a visit from Sonel and Craig the past few days has been a real treat. It was a joy to be with them as we took in some of the sights and ate dinner at one of our favorite Mexican restaurants. You really appreciate your children even more when you haven't seen them in a long time. With their hectic work schedules, I'm grateful that they were able to visit.

Your emails and cards continue to brighten my day, bringing a smile to my face, and even a few hardy laughs. I am truly touched by your thoughtfulness. I wish we could connect with all of you during our time in Baltimore, but this time we'll only be seeing our immediate family. I hope you understand.

All the best,

Susan

35

A Bell-Ringing Triumph

THE EMERGENCE OF SPRING, WITH its colorful blossoming beauty and warmer temperatures, brought a new vitality to our community, even for those who were still struggling with the effects of their treatments. For many, daily walks outdoors became the norm, bringing an inner peace that many thought would be unattainable a few months before.

Linwood graciously offered to give Chuck and me a tour of the Arnold Arboretum of Harvard University located in Jamaica Plain, a 265-acre park located not far from Hope Lodge. This magnificent area is a place for the public to enjoy, where there are thousands of species of shrubs and trees from North America, Asia, and Europe, all grouped by plant family and labeled with their name and country of origin. Many areas were just breathtaking, reviving my senses with nature's splendor.

None of us were up for walking the entire park, especially me, since I was beginning to experience skin irritation and redness on my buttocks from my radiation treatments. Consequently, we took short strolls and moved the car several times to visit the specific areas Linwood wanted us to see. His passion and knowledge of botany astounded us, but more importantly, we were seeing another side of Linwood—a healthier and more energized side, so different from when we first met.

Exhausted and yet still invigorated, we returned to Hope Lodge and found out that a twelve-year-old boy from Kosovo and his father were the newest guests. We learned the boy, Velimer, had been diagnosed with leukemia at age eight. An American family had sponsored him to come to the United States for help, but after three years of treatment his cancer had metastasized. At the time we met him at Hope Lodge, this young boy had not seen his family in Kosovo for years. His father, who barely spoke English and needed Velimer to translate for him, had flown to Boston to be with his son. How heartbreaking it must have been for Velimer to learn he was not going to go back to his family in Kosovo.

Most people at the Lodge went out of their way to be friendly and welcoming. It's tough enough for a child to deal with the ramifications of having cancer without seeing his mother for such a long time. Velimer's ordeal was much more difficult. You could see it in his eyes and in the anguish on his dad's face, which they both tried to hide. A group of us pitched in and bought them a gift card to Stop & Shop to buy groceries.

Hawk reached out to this family and took them under his wing, showed them the ropes, helped them with the language, and prepared a few meals for them. I overheard him talking to Velimer one morning, cautiously explaining his medical situation to him and what he now faced, carefully choosing his words, so he wouldn't frighten him anymore than he already was. Hawk's conversation with Velimer was extraordinary. Hawk continued to impress us with his thoughtfulness and compassion.

Ellie and Flora sort of adopted our new arrivals by sharing meals and taking them sightseeing and shopping. Ellie, who was only five years older than Velimer, could identify with his situation more than most of the adults. There didn't seem to be any barriers when they were together. She knew just how to reach out to him and they became good friends. Flora and Ellie's kindness created a wonderful bond between the two families that lasted long after Ellie and her Mom returned to California.

I continued to correspond with Ellie after returning home. Chuck and I later found out Velimer's father only had a temporary visa. Flora and her husband worked tirelessly to convince politicians to have his visa extended, which finally happened. Eventually, through the generosity of the Make-A-Wish Foundation, they were able to bring Velimer's whole family to America from Kosovo. What a homecoming that must have been!

Our time in Boston was winding down because Dr. Liebsch determined I needed five less treatments than he originally planned. Cindy and Barrie left a week before us. Those last hugs and goodbyes were especially tough. While the four of us had become close, it was Cindy and I who had built a unique, supportive friendship, one we both knew would last way beyond our time in Boston. It had only been two months since we first met; however, we could already read each other's minds and finish each other's sentences. We couldn't have lived further apart, with Cindy in upstate New York and me in Southwest Florida, yet we knew that the geographical distance between us couldn't keep us apart.

Although we were excited to be going home, it was hard saying good-bye to my proton and oncology teams, to Paul, and especially to Dr. Liebsch and Kathy. It was even harder saying good-bye to the staff at the Hope Lodge and the new friends we were leaving behind.

Flora and Ellie, who would still be staying at Hope Lodge after we left, took me out for an all-girl's fun day. During our subway ride, I listened to Ellie chatter about school, her boyfriend, and her amazing summers in Greece, and I enjoyed the pictures of Greece she showed me on her IPhone. In a relaxing atmosphere, we opened up about our journeys, exchanging details others wouldn't understand. In the middle of a fabulous lunch at the Cheesecake Factory, Flora received a phone call from her mother in Greece. She wanted to tell her daughter she had gone to the monastery in Greece to light candles for Ellie and me. I was humbled and touched by her thoughtfulness and concern.

My lavender spiral notebook was filled with addresses and phone numbers of people we had met. Everyone said they would keep in touch, but in actuality, I knew the ones who truly would, and those who would eventually drift apart. Many would be returning home to pick up the pieces of their former lives, others were in a "wait and see" pattern, and a few weren't sure what their next step would be, since their treatment or trial had not been successful. Regardless of their circumstances, everyone was immensely grateful for the AstraZeneca Hope Lodge and the American Cancer Society whose compassion and generosity had benefited so many.

April 21

Hi Family and Friends,

Yesterday I rang the bell at the Proton Center, signifying the completion of my treatment. I received a diploma from both the Proton and Radiation Oncology Centers. My son Scott said, "I bet you didn't think you'd get a diploma at your age!!" It was a very emotional experience. Dr. Liebsch decided I needed only 35, not 40 treatments. These gifted people have done all they can to keep the tumor from growing back. We are so grateful.

Our joy was bittersweet, clouded by the death of a guest at the Hope Lodge yesterday morning, a fifty-seven year old husband and father of two, twenty something year old sons. So glad our Hope Lodge family was here to support his wife.

So tomorrow we are flying to Baltimore. We'll drive to Frederick to visit with Bridget and Scott and see their new home. Then we'll drive to Richmond to be with Chuck's children, grandsons and family, celebrate Will's first communion, and catch all the sporting events for the five guys. We'll head back to Baltimore the first week in May to see Sonel and Craig's new home and check in with Dr. Wolinsky at

Hopkins. We leave for Sarasota on May 10. Can't wait to sleep in our own bed, and get back into a more normal routine.

We have had such a phenomenal experience in Boston. Our Hope Lodge family will always be a part of our most cherished memories. Their friendship, support, love, and laughter helped us get through this long tough journey. So we're going back home to live our lives and to finally publish my book.

Thanks for your love and support. You are the best!

Blessings and love to all of you.

Susan and Chuck

P.S. The Director of Hope Lodge suggested I frame the following poem I wrote and put it on a shelf in the first floor library, as encouragement for new guests as they begin their Boston journey.

They come—
by car, plane, train
from across the country
around the world
to Boston's premier cancer centers,
anticipating treatment
wondering about the future.

They find—
an extraordinary, caring place
a home away from home
new friendships
guidance and support
within its beautiful walls
a place of hope and healing…

at The American Cancer Society's
Hope Lodge.

Epilogue

This is not the end of the story. It usually never is after a cancer diagnosis. It's just the completion of my radiation treatments. I will continue to have MRIs and follow-up appointments every six months to a year, for a very long time (maybe the rest of my life), to make sure my tumor doesn't grow back. I really never think about it growing back until I am inside the MRI scanner. It's then that I wonder—*is this going to be the time?*

As hard as you try, some things are impossible to put behind you, even as life rolls forward. I have worked hard not to let the chordoma define who I am or kill my dreams. Yet, as I sought to return to some semblance of my former life, my brain had already begun to sort my life's journey into two categories; *BC*, my life *before the chordoma* and *AC,* my life *after the chordoma.*

Even with all the positive reinforcement I was consciously cramming into my brain, my mind still managed to have these two distinct divisions. I made a decision to place my whole focus and energy on making my "after" even better than my "before." I still have a lot of living to do, a "bucket list" to try to fulfill, and aspirations to achieve. I realize that some days I might not have complete control over what my mind is saying, but I also realize that I have the power within me to nurture my own growth and let God worry about the rest.

Cancer has taught me a lot about myself. I have learned that a positive attitude and acceptance are powerful tools when facing adversity. Sarah Ban Breathnach in her book, *Simple Abundance:*

a Daybook of Comfort and Joy, emphasizes how important it is to "accept and bless your circumstances." She writes:

> Acceptance is surrendering to what is: our circumstances, our feelings, our problems, our financial status, our work, our health, our relationships with other people, the delay of our dreams. Before we can change anything in our life, we have to recognize that this is the way it's meant to be *right now.*

Hopefully with time, circumstances will change for the better, yet no one knows when and if that will happen; but for *right now* it's your reality. How we channel our emotions, where we put our focus, how we educate ourselves, and the strategies we build upon are key in accepting our circumstances, moving forward. No one is prepared for a diagnosis of any type of cancer, but when I was able to accept my reality and rid myself of any negative thinking about worst case scenarios and those self-imposed mind images, I was able to move forward.

Having a life-changing event like cancer helped me see the bigger picture. I realize my journey would not have been a success without my amazing medical teams both at Johns Hopkins and Massachusetts General, and without a considerable amount of Divine intervention. I do not believe I am more religious than I was before my journey started, since my values and beliefs are still the same. I do know I am definitely more spiritual; savoring the simple pleasures, being more aware of the little miracles which occur each day, appreciating the people and beauty that surrounds me, taking less for granted, and cherishing all the blessings I have been given.

And I have truly been blessed. *Susie and Me Days: Joy in the Shadow of Dementia,* was finally published and put me on a new path, one which has enriched my life through speaking engagements and travel. Within a year after leaving Boston, our family grew from five grandsons to eight grandchildren, with the birth of three beautiful granddaughters. They are our jewels, our treasures; the ones whose energy, inquisitiveness, and uniqueness enrich our lives whenever we see them. This *truly* isn't the end of my story. It's been over five years with no recurrence of the chordoma. At my last appointment with Dr. Wolinsky, Chuck and I had the opportunity and privilege to meet Dr. Alfredo Quiñones-Hinojosa, a Professor of Neurosurgery and Oncology, Neuroscience and Cellular and Molecular Medicine and the Director of the Brain Tumor Surgery Program at Johns Hopkins Bayview Hospital and the Pituitary Surgery Program at the Johns Hopkins Hospital. His passion and commitment for helping others was evident as he described his interest in brain cancer and skull-based chordomas. Dr. Q leads a team of twenty-five other scientists funded by the National Institutes of Health, who work tirelessly in his Neurosurgery Brain Tumor Stem Cell Laboratory, better known as Dr. Q's Lab, trying to understand and unlock the mystery behind the development of chordomas.

Before my surgery, I had signed a release form giving Hopkins permission to use my tumor for research. *What was I going to do with it? Sell it on eBay?* Dr. Q enthusiastically told us his team was able to grow chordoma cells from my tumor, the *only one* that had been successful after many exhausting years of trying. Developing a cell line that would continue to grow for years to come, having the potential to benefit other scientists globally was a remarkable medical breakthrough. I was honored Dr. Q took the time to meet with us and thrilled I was contributing to his ground-breaking research. I knew I had been given a gift, but now it has real potential to become a gift for others.

Life is often full of maze-like paths, filled with twists, turns, and detours which can often complicate and change our lives in an instant. Yet, if we consciously watch for openings as we journey through the maze of life, and seize upon them as opportunities for self-examination and growth, they become a time to reflect and appreciate the simple things which we have been blessed with.

The poem, "Choice Lesson," in its elegant simplicity, captures the essence of my thoughts:

Growth brings change.
Unpredictable change.
Which can bring
Hesitancy to optimism.
It is essential that we cope
With the realities of the past
And the uncertainties of the future
With pure and chosen hope.
Not a blind faith,
But a strengthened choice.
Then, we can have the
Fortitude and wisdom necessary
To integrate life's many lessons
That collect beyond the points in time.
Growing like this will help
Build a good future,
For individuals,
For communities,
And for the world.

Mattie J.T. Stepaneck
Age 10
From "Hope through Heartsongs"

Resources

Chordoma Foundation:
http://www.chordomafoundation.org

Neurosurgical Spine Center at Johns Hopkins Hospital
http://www.hopkinsmedicine.org/neurology_neurosurgery/centers_clinics/spine/

The Massachusetts General Hospital Francis H. Burr Proton Therapy Center
http://www.massgeneral.org/radiationoncology/BurrProtonCenter.aspx

American Cancer Society
http://www.cancer.org

About the Author

A native of Baltimore, Maryland, and a retired kindergarten teacher, Susan found her muse at the Renaissance Institute at Notre Dame of Maryland University, a non-credit college for people over fifty. Never having embraced writing in high school or college, she began writing poetry, prose, and haiku, which ultimately led her to write her first book, *Susie and Me Days: Joy in the Shadow of Dementia.* Susan finds writing both stimulating and therapeutic. Now that her second book, *Confronting Chordoma Cancer: An Uncommon Journey* has been published, she is considering challenging herself again by delving into writing books for children.

In addition to writing, Susan is a volunteer support group facilitator for the Alzheimer's Association, Florida Gulf Coast Chapter. She has committed to become a volunteer peer guide as part of the Chordoma Foundation Peer Connect mentoring program. Susan is the mother of two sons, and stepmother to a son and daughter. She and her husband have eight grandchildren, and currently reside in Sarasota, Florida.

A portion of the profits from this book will go to support the Chordoma Foundation. This non-profit organization is working to improve the lives of chordoma patients by accelerating research to develop effective treatments for chordoma, and by helping patients to get the best care possible.

Visit Susan's web site: www.susanlgarbett.com
Watch Susan's story with her Johns Hopkins physicians:
http://bit.ly/hopkins-susans-story

19646580R00152

Made in the USA
Middletown, DE
29 April 2015